The
Short Story
Readers' Advisory

ALA READERS' ADVISORY SERIES

The Romance Readers' Advisory:
The Librarian's Guide to Love in the Stacks

The Short Story Readers' Advisory

A GUIDE TO THE BEST

Brad Hooper

American Library Association
Chicago and London
2000

Project editor: Louise D. Howe

Cover design: Design Solutions

Text design: Dianne M. Rooney

Composition by ALA Editions in Berkeley and Novarese using QuarkXpress 4.04 on a Macintosh platform

Printed on 50-pound white offset, a pH-neutral stock, and bound in 10-point coated cover stock by McNaughton & Gunn

The paper used in this publication meets the minimum requirements of American National Standard for Information Sciences—Permanence of Paper for Printed Library Materials, ANSI Z39.48-1992. ∞

Library of Congress Cataloging-in-Publication Data

Hooper, Brad.
    The short story readers' advisory : a guide to the best / by Brad Hooper.
        p. cm.
    Includes indexes.
    ISBN 0-8389-0782-2 (alk. paper)
       1. Libraries—United States—Special collections—Short stories.
    2. Readers' advisory services—United States. 3. Short stories—
    Bibliography. 4. Short stories, English—Bibliography. I. Title

    Z711.5 .H66 2000
    028′.9—dc21   99-085751

Printed in the United States of America.

04   03   02   01   00   5   4   3   2   1

Contents

Acknowledgments

I wish to thank Ben Segedin for his kindness in putting his computer skills to use in making the manuscript of this book happen. Also, thanks to Jim O'Laughlin for his suggestions and support.

1

The Short Story

An Appreciation and
a Definition

My seventh-grade language arts teacher, Mrs. Atkinson, looked like any other junior-high teacher in a small town in the Midwest in the early 1960s. But she had a vision and a creativity when it came to teaching that bestowed distinction upon her. Other teachers of her time and place seemed to have established safe and predictable routines beyond which they had no intention of venturing. They wanted the teaching day to be predictable and without surprises. Every year's curriculum looked just like last year's, and it would be the same the following year. But such mechanical teaching was not for Mrs. Atkinson. One of her above-and-beyond-the-call-of-duty choices for stimulating us, her students, was this: One day she tossed aside the reading textbooks we were supposed to use and ordered for each of us, through the good offices of *Scholastic* magazine, a copy of a selection of Edgar Allan Poe short stories. "Let's take on the *real* world of literature," she said, leading us there. And what a world the Poe tales plunged us into: haunting in its macabre situations, sophisticated and mysterious in its language. We grappled with his prose, we wrestled with it, and we came away glowing with self-satisfaction. "Aren't we something, mastering Poe?"

It was the intensity of their effect that left me shaken as I read those incomparable stories. Each story delivered a swift stab to my heart; each story was a stiletto blade piercing my vitals. Certainly,

I could not describe those sensations so metaphorically back then, but, looking back, I know those were my reactions to "The Tell-Tale Heart," "The Murders in the Rue Morgue," and "The Cask of Amontillado." All done fast and clean, a jolt of stimulation. And a shock of recognition, for in the space of a few pages and a few minutes we were offered quick but indelible glimpses into Poe's dark characters; and, as much as our seventh-grade experience level could aid us, he offered us peeks at the possibilities of darkness in our own souls.

"Intensity," "swift stab," "stiletto blade," "piercing," "fast and clean," "jolt," "shock." Notice the words I've used to describe my reactions to Poe. And when I reread him these days, I still use those words to convey their effect on me.

Furthermore, I often employ those words in sharing with other people how *all* short stories touch me.

Stories vs. Novels

One of my rules of thumb is "less is more." I prefer a little, quiet watercolor over a big, busy oil canvas any day. As diamonds result from the compression of coal, concentration tends to beget sublimity. Now, the warm accumulation of detail in reading a good novel is a wonderful thing, there is no doubt; but the pleasure of the quick, concentrated reading experience is more piquant, or so I feel. Fans of novels often say they love to "live" in a novel for an extended period of time, like taking a long vacation by the sea in that you know tomorrow will bring more joy and contentment, and the dreary return to work lies way off in the future.

Well, then, reading a short story is like a day trip as opposed to an extended vacation. I remember a day trip out of London, my destination Salisbury; in a few short hours I'd left the bustle of London completely behind (it is a city I adore, don't get me wrong) and found myself elevated into a state of grace by the absolute beauty of Salisbury Cathedral, a sensation that floods over me again and again whenever I get out my photo albums or happen to see in some book or other a reproduction of a Constable watercolor of the cathedral. I have always thought afterwards that a lengthier stay in Salisbury might have lessened the impact of the cathedral on my esthetic sensibilities.

And think about this: How would the impact on the reader of that "thump-thump" of the beating heart in Poe's "A Tell-Tale Heart" have been diluted if Poe had dragged out the build-up of that incredibly creepy sensation to fill the pages of a novel?

The overarching point I'm making is that there is room for both: the long vacation and the day trip, the novel and the short story. Each has its place in a person's schedule and in his or her needs to nourish the soul. The rewards differ, of course, and both should be experienced.

Fiction readers often indicate a "fear" of the short story. "I don't *get* them" is a common response. The fear of not "getting" a short story seems to be based on some sort of notion that short stories are like fables, in that each one is supposed to lead to some obvious, concluding lesson about life. But what makes them even more challenging than fables, according to this line of thinking, is that the lesson about life taught by a short story is not clearly spelled out like the moral of a fable; it is left vague, requiring readers to spell it out for themselves. Readers fear, then, that they won't come up with the "right" lesson or won't be able to discern any lesson at all.

Librarians, it's time to disabuse your fiction-loving but short-story-fearing readers of such notions! Granted, the reader of a short story may have to work a little harder at paying attention, for, while most everything the reader needs to know in a novel is spelled out, in a short story much is simply implied or suggested. But there is no more a "lesson" to be learned from a short story than there is from a novel; both allow readers to witness—one briefly, the other in lengthier fashion—human beings trying to lead their lives. Both—short stories and novels—are there for readers to get out of them what they can, and what they *do* get out of reading a short story or a novel is pure benefit in terms of learning about—as clichéd as it seems—life!

Don't fear the short story. Don't approach one as though you're going to have to "figure it out." Just let it wash over you and pique your sensations. That's what short stories do: pique your sensations.

Short Stories Today

In the last two decades of the twentieth century, the short story in the United States has experienced a renaissance. Publishing interest and readership interest have steadily increased. The short-story collection is no longer a literary pariah. Collections of stories now enjoy big print runs, considerable publicity campaigns on the part of publishers, and receipt of literary prizes (on many occasions, over novels also up for consideration). Yes, most story writers still write novels; publishers still want the revenue a novel can generate over a story collection; and, let's face it, the conviction still exists that a fiction writer has not truly "arrived" without having written a novel. But it is also true that extremely talented fiction writers are not simply churning out short stories during idle hours between writing novels. Instead, they focus their talent on the writing of stories as much as they do on their novels—and, in many cases, more so.

What are the reasons behind the short-story renaissance that began in the 1980s (and will continue to flourish well into the next century, it is hoped)? No one has yet come up with the perfect answer. Suggestions float about; they center on two points. One, that in this highly technological, fast-paced society, the short story is perfectly suited to the fragmented reading time available to us in our busy days. Two, that the proliferation of graduate-level university writing programs has resulted in writers who, on a regular basis, are capable of filling publishers' mailboxes to the brim with envelopes containing quite publishable material.

Defining the Short Story

Before launching ourselves onto the high seas of discussing specific steps in short-story readers' advisory, it would be helpful to librarians who are readers of short stories as well as librarians *helping* readers of short stories to ponder the definition and characteristics of the form.

Just what is a short story, then?

Most people would answer that it is a piece of fiction much shorter than a novel.

5

THE SHORT STORY

While that response is true, more than just length separates the short story from the novel.

As most of us know, Edgar Allan Poe was an important American short-story writer, and, as I've stated previously, one who had a great influence on my appreciation for the short-story form. In a review of Nathaniel Hawthorne's short-story collection *Twice-Told Tales* (published in 1837), Poe issued what has become a classic position paper on the definition of the short story.

> As the novel cannot be read at one sitting, it cannot avail itself of the immense benefit of *totality*. Worldly interests, intervening during the pauses of perusal, modify, counteract, and annul the impressions intended. But simply cessation in reading would, of itself, be sufficient to destroy the true unity. In the brief tale, however, the author is enabled to carry out his full design without interruption. During the hours of perusal, the soul of the reader is at the writer's control.
>
> A skilful artist has constructed a tale. He has not fashioned his thoughts to accommodate his incidents, but having deliberately conceived a certain *single effect* to be wrought, he then invents such incidents, he then combines such events, and discusses them in such a tone as may best serve him in establishing this preconceived effect. If his very first sentence tends not to the out-bringing of this effect, then in his very first step has he committed a blunder. In the whole composition there should be no word written of which the tendency, direct or indirect, is not to the one pre-established design. And by such means, with such care and skill, a picture as at length painted which leaves in the mind of him who contemplates it with a kindred art, a sense of the fullest satisfaction. The idea of the tale, its thesis, has been presented unblemished, because undisturbed—an end absolutely demanded, yet, in the novel, altogether unattainable.[1]

That remains the best definition, I feel, of the short story—different from a novel in that it is short enough to be read in one sitting, with *every* word leading toward some final, preordained effect.

---

1. Ann Charters, ed., *The Story and Its Writer: An Introduction to Short Fiction* (New York: St. Martin's, 1983), pp. 1123–24.

In chapter 2, I will introduce and explain a system whereby librarians can help library patrons connect to the world of the short story, a system I dub "total commitment" readers' advisory. Its framework is the six basic elements of fiction found in both the novel and the short story, namely: *plot, theme, style, character, setting,* and *point of view.* These are the "reader hooks" of any piece of fiction; some aspect of one of these elements, or two of them, or all of them, is what catches the reader's attention and carries her or him through to the end; determining which of the elements has done so is the basic premise of "total commitment" readers' advisory.

Following the chapter on readers' advisory, are two chapters offering capsule critical essays on one hundred fifty outstanding short-story writers past and present; familiarity with these authors will afford both you the librarian and your fiction-reading patrons a wonderful working knowledge of the field of the short story.

2

"Total Commitment" Readers' Advisory

Now let us explore a readers' advisory program that I feel is suitable for use with all library patrons who desire to connect their reading interests with the world of the short story.

The Basic Sources

Of course, the first place to turn to help library patrons who are interested in reading short stories to locate a certain type or types of short story they may feel comfortable reading, or a particular short story by a certain author they may have heard about, is to the basic reference sources available in most public libraries. These include *Short Story Index, Short Story Criticism, Directory of Literary Biography, The Readers' Advisor, Reference Guide to Short Fiction, Chicorel Index to Short Stories in Anthologies,* and *Index to Short Stories.*

This is the most direct way to connect readers with short stories; it's also the least imaginative. It's a quick and easy method for the librarian: library patrons can simply be pointed in the direction of those sources and told to use them themselves according to the guidelines presented in the front of each volume, "and if you encounter any difficulties or problems, then come back to the desk for further assistance." However, as should be obvious, this is a sure way to lose a patron's interest and desire for short-story reading! How many general readers want to pore over the pages of reference tools?

Of course, any good librarian worth his or her salt will accompany patrons to the reference shelves and show them how to use these sources, helping patrons come up with a list of short-story titles to seek out in the stacks, either still in their original periodical form or having been republished within the pages of a collection.

A relatively neat and tidy process, isn't it? Done without much fuss—but also without much passion on the part of the librarian!

What library patrons really want is a more personal touch. They want you, the librarian, to make an individual match between their reading interests and appropriate reading materials, particularly if they have enjoyed a short story they found on their own and now want to find other short stories they will enjoy.

And the "personal touch" is the fun of readers' advisory, to say nothing of being the most effective and productive kind of help to a library patron. What ingenuity and knowledge does it require for a librarian to point to a set of reference books and say "Go find a story you might like in there?"

But what rewarding fun it can be to immerse yourself in short stories and then get totally involved in your patrons' interests in that area! And what rewards await your library patron who subsequently can take advantage of your commitment!

READERS' ADVISORY TIP 1

Building and Maintaining a Short Story Collection

- First, appraise your holdings to determine what short-story writers are represented and what collections of their work are in your collection. Then draw up a *desiderata* list using the capsule critical essays in this book, including as many short-story writers as your fiction budget will accommodate.

- All regular book-review sources review new and forthcoming short-story collections, including *Booklist*, *Library Journal*, and *Publishers Weekly*. Newspaper book-review sections, particularly the *New York Times Book Review*, devote a lot of space to reviews of new books of short stories.

■ Among the most helpful features in newspaper book-review sections, at least in terms of short-story collection development, are combined reviews of more than one book of short stories. These combined reviews are excellent for helping the librarian determine which of the books of stories would be most suitable for addition to your fiction collection. For instance, if your library is located in Mississippi, a book of short stories set in the South probably would have priority of purchase over collections reviewed along with it that are set in other parts of the country.

■ To practice truly conscientious short-story selection, however, librarians should go beyond basic review sources and regularly consult "specialty" sources. That is, check as many literary journals as you have access to, because they all offer on a regular basis very professional reviews not only of novels and books of literary criticism and biography but also of short-story collections. The premier literary journal to consult is the scholarly journal devoted to the short-story form, *Studies in Short Fiction*. Other literary journals to consult for reviews of short-story collections include *Southern Review*, *Georgia Review*, *Tri-Quarterly*, and *The Gettysburg Review*.

■ Keep an eye on publishers' catalogs, particularly from Penguin, to keep yourself apprised not only of what new short-story collections are coming out but also of what is available on publishers' backlists. Frequently, these backlisted titles are just the ticket for filling blank spots on your short-story shelves to ensure that you have a well-rounded collection of all the important short-story writers past and present.

■ Weed those crummy looking short-story collections out of your library. Of course, if a sorry-looking tome happens to be the only way a certain writer can still be represented on your shelves—that is, if no new and better-looking edition is available—then by all means keep it. But if the old, ratty volumes can be replaced by spanking new ones, even if the replacements are paperback, then make that switch. Patrons reluctant to read short stories to begin with are certainly not going to be stimulated to do so by torn, ugly binding and yellowed pages. Also, pay attention to the publication of someone's "collected" or "complete" short stories; the new availability of that writer's entire short-story output in one volume affords you the opportunity to weed out all previous collections. Why not have the new and handsomely bound "collected" or "complete" volume on your shelf instead of the older and probably tired-looking volumes it can replace.

There is no substitute for achieving "total commitment" readers' advisory capability by securing a solid reading background in the short story yourself. An undergraduate degree in literature, or even a second master's degree in literature, does not promise extensive exposure to short stories. It is an undertaught genre. Knowing short stories and short-story writers is almost always a matter of self-education. Simply put, you've got to teach yourself short stories.

The best place to start is, of course, this book you have in hand right now. Read and study all the entries in the next two chapters, take notes, and read the stories I've suggested within each author entry.

READERS' ADVISORY TIP 2

Taking Notes

Take notes about the short stories and short-story writers you read on index cards and keep the cards in a file box. Or have a loose-leaf notebook or bound exercise book handy for inscribing your notes. Or maintain a computer file to call up, consult, or add to at will. Whatever format you are most comfortable with and find most convenient, *take notes on short stories*. Think of these notes as your readers' advisory ready-reference. Take notes based on the six elements of fiction listed in chapter 1: stories you've read that have a theme of adultery or of father-son conflict, for instance; stories that are set in the Midwest; stories that have plots featuring journeys or family gatherings. Cross-reference your entries: if a story is set in the West, for instance, list other stories with the same setting.

> The more notes you take on what you've read—and, of course, the more organized you are with your notes—the more useful a resource your notebook or card file or computer file will be to you in helping a patron connect with an appropriate short story.

Anthologies and Collections

The next place to turn in your self-education in the short story is anthologies: compilations of short stories by a variety of authors. Anthologies will familiarize you not only with other stories by writers discussed in this book but also with authors not included here.

Most often the stories in any particular anthology have been gathered together within the pages of one volume based on the compiler's vision of "best" in terms of theme, time period, or region. Some anthologies are "annual events"; these include *Best American Short Stories* and *New Stories from the South,* two estimable series published every year. Other anthologies, such as those discussed in the appendix of this book, are "one-time shots": published only once.

Read both kinds: the yearlies, to familiarize yourself with who is writing these days, writers who are not discussed in the entries that follow, and what they write about; and the "one-time" anthologies, particularly those that gather the best of times past, to acquaint yourself with writers of the past—again, ones that are not reviewed in this book—who were significant in the development of the short story.

Most anthologies present brief biographical sketches of the included authors. Pay attention to these sketches, for they usually impart information useful in readers' advisory: the author's nationality or regional background, important themes they have explored, and their other writings.

This book you have in your hand, as well as the anthologies you've located and studied, will steer you to writers that have appeal to you; seek out collections of these writers' works. A "collection" is a compilation of stories by a single author, as opposed to the anthology, which we have already defined as a compilation of stories by more than one author.

Then, voila! Here you are! You've educated yourself in the short story by studying this book and then examining several anthologies and subsequently seeking out collections of stories by the authors who interested you. It's not a course that can be accomplished overnight, by any means. It takes time, but give yourself over to it.

You will be surprised at and delighted by the variety of short stories out there: the variety of approaches to writing a short story and the flexibility of the form in accommodating the creative needs and desires of each and every author. The short story, you'll come to see, is not a brittle, narrow, little thing, thin and anemic and subject to breakage if not handled delicately. No, it is robust and resilient and capable of showing a thousand different sparkling faces, like the view through a kaleidoscope.

READERS' ADVISORY TIP 3

Hooking Genre Readers into Reading Short Stories

Readers who enjoy genre fiction should be encouraged to enjoy "genre" short stories. To a patron who enjoys mysteries, suggest that at those times when the crunch between job and driving the kids somewhere and pottery classes becomes too tight to stick with a novel without taking months to finish—thus perhaps losing its momentum and total effect—then what the doctor ordered is a collection of mystery short stories. These are compact pieces of crime and detection that, while satisfying the craving for murder, mayhem, and sleuthing, nonetheless can be wrapped up, completed, and enjoyed in toto in the few minutes slated for bolting down a sandwich on your office lunch break or while cooling your heels waiting for Junior's soccer practice to be over.

G. K. Chesterton's Father Brown stories are classics and remain timeless in their ability to provoke and charm. And, of course, a collection of Sherlock Holmes tales can't be beat. The American hard-boiled detective writers produced short stories as well as novel masterpieces; have your mystery-loving patrons try Dashiell Hammett, for instance. Little country-house cozies can be enjoyed in the anthology *English Country House Murders* (Mysterious Press, 1989). And a subscription to *Ellery Queen's Mystery Magazine* will provide plenty of fodder for mystery-loving patrons.

The same concept applies to steering science fiction lovers toward reading short stories. Appeal to their need to sustain their addiction to the genre by suggesting they try SF short stories in those odd moments of the day when starting and finishing a narrative piece at one sitting sounds appealing. Ray Bradbury is a remarkable short-story writer, so remarkably adept at fantasy that even the most reluctant short-story reader will be charmed into enjoying his work in the short form.

Of course, your immediate strategy here, as a short-story readers' advisor, is to get those genre readers hooked on genre short stories and thus, once they're comfortable with the form, easily encourage them to try "nongenre" short stories; for, as you know, a whole world of short stories about everything awaits them. They just need you to open the door for them.

Initiating Short-Story Readers' Advisory

Armed with your new-found knowledge of the short story, you are ready to engage in a set of procedures for connecting readers to short stories and short-story writers suitable to their reading interests.

The first procedure is to introduce your short-story interested library patrons to this book, letting them do as you did: examine it, take notes from it, read the stories cited herein, and use the indexes to nationality and subject found in the back of the book as directional tools for locating other stories that might interest them.

The second procedure in helping library patrons find stories suitable for their needs and interests is also one that you utilized in your self-education on the short story: the use of anthologies. Introduce your patrons to the anthologies you explored in your self-education. Matches between their reading tastes and the short stories they encounter in the anthologies may not be automatic, but certainly the anthologies give them room to explore possibilities for connecting their reading interests to certain short stories and short-story writers. Also, readers will undoubtedly encounter stories in anthologies they don't like; it would be helpful to the librarian to understand why they disliked a certain story yet liked another one.

READERS' ADVISORY TIP 4

Historical Short Fiction?

There's no such thing, for all practical purposes. Science fiction short stories, yes; mystery short stories, indeed; and even romance short stories. But the genre of historical fiction is for the most part limited to the novel form. You will rarely, rarely find a short story set in the distant past: distant from the time during which it was written, that is. Why? Who knows. It just seems that the short story is thought of by readers and editors alike as most suitable for reflecting contemporary life, or life as it was led in the very recent past.

The consequence of this situation for readers' advisory is that the relatively easy connective link for readers of mysteries or science fiction or romance from the novel to the short story will not be as likely a process when it comes to readers of historical fiction.

The answer to this problem is, though, to suggest to historical novel lovers that they might enjoy reading short stories *written* in the past, as a way of helping to satisfy their reading appetite for fictional visits to yesteryear. A reader who likes fiction that evokes the old days will enjoy the short stories of, say, Henry James; even though his immaculate depictions of social customs of the late nineteenth century were *written* at the time they depict, reading them now gives a sense of reading historical fiction.

Ah, the virtues of sleight of hand! It's *all* about attempting to get all of your fiction lovers to read short stories as well as novels, isn't it?

Focusing on the Elements of Short Stories

The third procedure is the real "heart" of the short-story readers' advisory program. This procedure is certainly the most involving and elaborate. It centers on the "reference interview": questions to ask a patron that will lead to making a successful reader-story connection.

These questions focus on the six basic elements of fiction:

> plot
>
> theme
>
> style
>
> character
>
> setting
>
> point of view

The librarian can lead patrons into recognizing how short-story writers may emphasize one or two of these elements over the other ones, and help them to recognize which elements appeal to them most in a particular short story they have enjoyed; this, in turn, will lead to finding other short stories emphasizing the same one or two elements.

READERS' ADVISORY TIP 5

Warning: Don't Make a Face

My Psychology 101 class in college was taught by a woman who had many colorful ways of expressing herself and making points. Once she told us about a study showing a connection between a mother's facial expression and her child's reception of the medicine she was administering to him or her. It seems that a frown or a grimace on the mother's face as she extended the spoonful of medicine automatically set up an expectation of foul taste on the part of the child.

Remember the result of that study. What does that have to do with readers' advisory, I can hear you asking! Well, you as a librarian may, after learning short stories and short-story readers' advisory inside and out, decide that you don't really care for the form. Understand it, yes, and even appreciate it; but not really like it. It's novels for you, you decide.

And that's fine, for there is no law that says you have to like short stories. *But just remember not to prejudice your fiction-reading patrons.* Don't grimace when you're conducting a short-story readers' advisory session. Seriously, now; some adverse comments about short stories said to someone making tentative steps toward learning about short stories could discourage him or her from taking any further steps.

Plot

To begin your interview with a short-story-reading patron, or one who is interested in becoming a short-story reader, you will want to discuss, first, *plot*. Now, of course, the plot of a short story is not as involved as the plot usually found in a novel, but most short stories do indeed have a plot. It may be as simple as someone encountering an old friend on the street. And the plot of a story should be relatively simple, for complicated plots are best left to the larger playing field of the novel.

Let's say a patron expresses having enjoyed a short story by Stephen Crane. The story, you find out, is entitled "The Open Boat." Yes, a very famous short story, frequently anthologized; and in your "self-education" in the short story, you have undoubtedly read it yourself by now.

Ask the patron what happens in this short story—not every detail of the plot line, but in basic terms. You and the patron will agree that the story is about a shipwreck, plain and simple.

The question to ask, then, is "Do you want another short story about a shipwreck? Is it the *plot* of this short story the element that got you hooked, and do you want another one with a similar plot?"

It is entirely possible that, yes, it *is* the plot that was the major hook, and, *yes*, the patron does indeed want more stories about shipwreck.

Theme

Chances are, though, that what the patron is interested in pursuing is more short stories that share a similar *theme* to "The Open Boat." Nine times out of ten, patrons, when interviewed about a short story they enjoyed and what they would like to read next, will divulge that what they really want is a short story with a similar theme rather than a similar plot.

But getting readers to identify the theme of a short story they have read and enjoyed probably will be more difficult than getting them to explain the plot. Unless a reader has had exposure to literature classes, labeling a theme is not a comfortable exercise for them. It is going to take experience on your part to help boil a story down to its thematic underpinnings.

But, getting back to "The Open Boat," here's where your new-found expertise in short stories comes into play. You suggest to the reader that in thematic terms, "The Open Boat" is about survival in the face of harsh elements. And is that what you liked about it? you ask. Is that what moved you in this particular short story? "Yes," will be the probable answer; a reader's response to this short story usually has to do with being moved by its "survival" motif rather than the fact of the shipwreck. In fact, most readers' responses to a short story are usually more connected to its theme rather than its plot.

"Good," you say. "In that case, I have another very interesting short story about survival in the elements, a much more contemporary story that you may respond to even more enthusiastically." You place in the patron's hands the Rick Bass story "Choteau." The narrator of this bold story has a friend, Jim, who likes to hunt in a remote part of Canada. "The tiny dirt road going into Canada hugs a mountain face on one side," relates the narrator, "and the sheerest of cliffs on the other. Driving it, if you dare, you can look down and see the nauseating white spills of rapids in the Moyle River."

Let the patron take this story home, and chances are he or she will return to the library as a fan of the adventure stories of Rick Bass, one of our best contemporary short-story writers. If the patron returns to the desk not only wanting more Bass stories but also wanting other authors' stories with a survival-against-the-elements theme, then it's an easy step from Bass to two "classic" American short-story writers, Jack London and Ernest Hemingway.

Any number of Jack London's stories qualify here in terms of theme, as do several of Ernest Hemingway's short stories, including "The Short Happy Life of Francis Macomber," which features Robert Wilson, a white hunter in Africa, who is an archetypical Hemingway hero leading a manly life of action.

Style

Now let us turn to the third element of fiction we listed above: *style*. And let's go back to the library patron who enjoyed Stephen Crane's short story "The Open Boat." Crane wrote in a style of yesterday: it is precise and clean but a little more elaborate and embellished than, say, that of Rick Bass, whose style is rock-hard in its compactness, flinty in its diamond-tough flawlessness.

If what the patron liked most about the Crane story was "the writing," then he or she paid attention to the writer's style and responded to it. That is a good indication that this person would prefer to stick with short-story writers of the past, rather than delve into the relatively cleaner writing of today. Your suggestions to this patron can be tailored accordingly: read writers contemporaneous to Crane. These are easy to locate, simply by checking the birth and death dates of the authors listed in the "Masters of the Past" chapter of this book.

Character

The aspect of *character* must now draw our consideration: the fourth of the six basic elements of fiction. This, however, is one of the two least important factors in determining whether a reader enjoyed a certain short story. Certainly, the reader may respond to a short story by saying, "I really enjoyed the main character," or, "Boy, I couldn't stand that character." But character—or character *type,* to be more specific—is not really a strong connective bridge from one short story to another. For example, few library patrons who have read, say, Eudora Welty's incomparable story "Death of a Traveling Salesman," will ask a librarian to please locate another story about a traveling salesman.

If, however, you *do* have a patron who wants stories featuring certain character types, here is where your own personal knowledge of the field of the short story will have to come strongly into play. If a patron wants stories only about, say, nurses, relying on your memory to come up with answers will be very helpful; and in preparation for such requests, remember the importance of maintaining a file— either a computer file or a card file—based on character types: "nurses," "traveling salesmen," "eccentric old ladies," etc.

On the other hand, if a patron responded strongly to "The Death of a Traveling Salesman"—and few readers will fail to respond to it— his or her response is probably based more on a connection to the *theme* of sickness and death, or to Welty's unique *style,* or this story's rural southern *setting.*

Setting

Setting, it must be said, may well be the most important factor in connecting a reader to a short story. "You enjoyed Sherwood Anderson's depiction of small-town midwestern life in *Winesburg, Ohio?*" you may find yourself asking a patron who informs you of how much pleasure they derived from this classic cycle of short stories.

"And you want other short stories set in the small-town Midwest?" you will ask them.

"Try the lovely short stories, then, of William Maxwell, who grew up in Lincoln, Illinois, and writes about that town with particular poignancy."

Or your interview with the potential short-story loving reader may run along lines like these:

"So, you are an urban dweller; do you want to read stories set in big cities?

"If so, start with the New York stories of Deborah Eisenberg, who knows that terrain like the proverbial back of her hand."

Or, "Do you enjoy travel? If overseas travel is an important part of your life, you may want short stories by writers from other countries, or perhaps by American writers who often write about foreign lands.

"If the latter category interests you, I would recommend the short stories of Kay Boyle, who lived many years as an expatriate and wrote about her experiences with particular discernment and richness."

Connecting readers to setting is important, but, actually, it is one of the easiest connections a librarian can make from one short story to another. There is relatively little ambiguity about identifying setting, at least general types of setting, as compared to theme identification or even style identification.

Point of View

The sixth basic element of fiction is *point of view*. Most successful short stories have *one* point of view; the confined space, the necessity for a strong, clean, central effect in a short story, more or less prohibits multiple points of view.

But most general readers don't worry about point of view. It's not going to be a connective factor from one short story to another, at least in terms of the ordinary readers'-advisory situations you will find yourself in. Pay attention to point of view when you're involved in your self-education in the short story, but realize it will not be a bridge you'll often use to connect patrons to short stories.

READERS' ADVISORY TIP 6

Practical Readers' Advisory Activities

■ Make a visually enticing display for serious fiction readers that is devoted exclusively to the short story. Put new collections by contemporary writers—particularly those collections with interesting jackets—out on display with a mix of some attractively bound paperback editions of classic short-story writers of yesterday. But, when it comes to choosing which classic writers, avoid those who immediately connote "genius thus dull," such as Chekhov, Kipling, and Borges. Instead, display writers whose names are bywords for entertainment, such as Saki, Erskine Caldwell, and Mark Twain.

■ Lead, or encourage fiction-loving patrons to organize, discussion groups for short stories. At the very least, suggest to discussion groups you know about, particularly ones that may initially have gotten together or actually meet in your library, that on a regular basis they include short-story collections in their round of books to discuss.

■ *Any* seasonal or thematic display of fiction should always include short-story collections as well as novels. If your display centers on suggested books for "hearthside reading in the depths of winter," display some "serious" short-story writers who really can be appreciated during quiet reading times, such as before a warming fire on a frigid afternoon. These writers could include Henry James, William Faulkner, Donald Barthelme, and William Trevor.

■ Whenever a collection of stories wins a big literary prize (and it *does* happen), such as the Pulitzer Prize, the National Book Award, or the National Book Critics' Circle Award, make a big deal of it in terms of display. Bring out from the shelves any of the author's previous collections, and involve yourself in "total commitment" readers' advisory by displaying along side the prize-winner's work other writers—"read alikes"—that connect in some fashion or other to the writer you are focusing on. If the prize winner is southern, bring out other southern writers past and present. The prize winner known for her stories of suburbanites? Get your John Cheever collection out and set it next to her. Displays like this are one excellent way to keep in practice for short-story readers' advisory.

READERS' ADVISORY TIP 7

Your Continuing Education

We spoke of educating yourself in the world of the short story as it pertains to becoming a learned, totally commited readers' advisor; and now we speak of a correlative issue: continuing your education in the short story. In a word, *do!* Do continue your own education. Even after your intense education in the form is essentially over, I would suggest a regimen such as this: never let a week pass without having read one or two short stories. Let them be a mix of stories you've found in book collections and stories you run across in such periodicals as the *New Yorker* and *North American Review*. The point is to keep abreast of who is writing what and how you can best share your enthusiasm with library patrons.

Summary

This guide to the short story emphasizes *writers* over individual *works*—although within each discussion, I cite an exemplary story or two or three. Locating the particular stories or editions or compilations cited here is less important than bringing to your attention the writers themselves. In most instances, the collection listed under each author is only a sample of what is in print. Let the books listed serve as a starting point. Familiarity with these men and women will make you conversant indeed in the short story.

3

Masters of the Past

The following men and women, none of whom is still living, are the masters who either contributed to the birth of the short story in what we perceive as its "modern" garb in the nineteenth century or were in the forefront of making it an even more integral literary form in the twentieth century. These are the writers whom I feel still retain the most appeal to contemporary readers, who are most relevant to anyone wanting to experience the artistic integrity of this literary form.

Alice Adams
American. 1926–1999.

Adams' focus was on women—often from academe, or artists and writers. In a tight, clean, brilliant style, without flamboyance, she dissected women's relations with men, particularly vis-à-vis female dependence on the material things and emotional sustenance males can provide. More specifically, Adams analyzed fears common to women: aloneness, physical pain, and the ability to react well to emotional stress, among others. Her stories are so deeply psychological that as much conflict goes on inside the characters' heads as takes place in the world around them. Correlative to her unadorned prose style, there is never any extravagance of plot or character, which only increases her stories' psychological potency. She is a thorough expert in narrative structure. "His Women" and "The Islands" are two characteristic stories.

Adams, Alice. *The Last Lovely City.* 208p. Knopf (0-679-45441-1).

Shmuel Yosef Agnon
Israeli. 1908–1970.

This 1966 Nobel Prize winner is one of the best, and best known, Hebrew writers. He preferred to write about the European Jewish diaspora: specifically, Jewish life as its past was reflected in its present. His stories, in their uncluttered prose style, and written with a tone of the traditional moral tale, celebrate Jewish values and traditions, most notably the bonds of family. Agnon used Hebrew legends, lore, customs, and rituals as the basis for his fiction, which can occasionally take on surreal, unreal, or dreamlike qualities. But he is not entirely upbeat in his stories, for they are often grounded, too, in a person's disconnection from real, true human nature. Within this thematic context, Agnon reflected on personal alienation from surroundings and the disorder individuals witness or perceive around them. And he treated with sensitivity the bipolarity of contemporary Jewish life: the tension between leading a religious life or a secular one. "A Whole Life" is a major Agnon story, presented in eleven short, numbered sections. The narrator "had not tasted anything all day long." Living alone in Jerusalem, his wife and children elsewhere, the man had prepared nothing on Sabbath eve to eat on the Sabbath; his intention was to go eat at a hotel, but before that can happen he is detained by a friend, who asks him to stop by the post office to mail a packet of important letters. The story follows his digressions before he is able to get to the hotel dining room, but securing a sustaining meal still eludes him. A marvelously wrought story on being torn between spiritual and earthly impulses.

Agnon, S. Y. *Twenty-One Stories.* 287p. Schocken; dist. by Random, paper (0-8052-0313-3).

Sherwood Anderson
American. 1876–1941.

Legend has it that one day in 1912, Anderson simply picked up and walked out of his Ohio paint factory to devote himself to writing.

Whether it happened exactly that way or not, in 1919 he produced a classic in *Winesburg, Ohio*, a cycle of interrelated stories that sympathetically viewed lonely and frustrated individuals in a fictitious midwestern town. Anderson's direct style influenced a generation of U.S. fiction writers, Hemingway and Faulkner among them; however, some readers may now find his writing occasionally simplistic and even unrefined. Nonetheless, Anderson could bore quickly, seemingly effortlessly, to the core of the Winesburgers' distress. *Winesburg* can be read straight through as a novel; or a few of the stories can be delved into and fully appreciated individually. The story "Hands" is both exemplary and the most affecting of those in the collection. It concerns a man who must keep hidden his fluttery hands, which once, because of their excessive expressiveness, got him into dire trouble.

Anderson, Sherwood. *Winesburg, Ohio*. 247p. Penguin, paper (0-14-018655-7).

Isaak Babel
Russian. 1894–1941.

Babel, the son of a Jewish merchant in Odessa, was a soldier in World War I and subsequently joined the Bolshevik organization. He died in a Stalinist labor camp, perhaps murdered. Babel is best known for stories based on his service with the Cossacks in Poland during the war, but he also wrote about life in the Jewish quarter of his native Odessa, particularly the criminal underground. The celebrated stories "Dolgushov's Death" and "Korol" are examples of both types, fully demonstrating Babel's characteristic stripped-of-modifiers style. He was a wonderful miniaturist, writing compactly, vividly, and beautifully, with every word delivering the effect of a carpenter's perfectly placed hammer blow on a nail head. His visual images are powerfully wrought; his characters jump alive from the page.

Babel, Isaak. *Collected Stories*. 363p. Penguin, paper (0-14-018462-7).

James Baldwin
American. 1924–1987.

Baldwin is magnificent. Not read as much as he was in the 1950s and 1960s, he nonetheless remains a major figure in modern American literature. Born and raised in Harlem, where his father was a preacher,

Baldwin himself practiced his father's profession in his younger life. He spent much of his adult life in Paris, to escape the racism he found in the United States. As well known for his essays as for his fiction, Baldwin, in both forms, illuminated the difficulties involved in the black individual establishing an identity not only in a dominant white society but also within the black community itself. Baldwin's writing voice, even with its angry pitch, never loses timbre and resonance. A line from his story "Sonny's Blues"—"One boy was whistling a tune, at once very complicated and very simple"—offers an apt description of Baldwin's own songfulness in airing basic human needs. "Sonny's Blues" is a riveting story about the relationship between a high school teacher in Harlem and his younger brother, Sonny, a jazz pianist.

Baldwin, James. *Going to Meet the Man.* 249p. Random/Vintage, paper (0-679-76179-9).

Toni Cade Bambara
American. 1939–1995.

Bambara grew up in a poor section of New York City, and her stories reflect that environment. She was college educated yet still street-smart, and the voice in her fiction is the colloquial one of urban blacks. Bambara was truly humorous but, at the same time, wise and realistic. Her stories of black life in the city, as well as those set in less urbanized locales, are often satiric, exploding stereotypes and pointing to ironies in the differences between generations. In addition, Bambara's use of metaphor is brilliant. All her strengths are on display in the title story of her collection *Gorilla, My Love.* The narrator, a little girl, is upset to learn that her beloved uncle is not really planning to marry her when she grows up. "Grownups figure," she decides, "they can treat you just anyhow. Which burns me up . . . . what with grownups playing change-up and turnin you round every which way so bad. And don't ever say they sorry."

Bambara, Toni. *Gorilla, My Love.* 177p. Random/Vintage, paper (0-679-73898-3).

Donald Barthelme
American. 1931–1989.

Until his death, Barthelme was the dean of contemporary U.S. experimental writers. His stories are difficult to grasp and they will infuriate many readers. His sardonic visions of contemporary society bear disjointed narratives—no straight linear progression from point *A* to point *Z*. His stories are akin to puzzles—fragments of dialogue and action and imagery are thrown at the reader, who then must piece them together into a cohesive entity. Political ineptitude, familial and sexual struggles, materialism, the impossibility of language to truly communicate experience: these are the themes of Barthelme's stories. Characters? All kinds of people, the identifiable as well as the unrecognizable. "The Indian Uprising" is a supreme challenge. This story may be seen as greatly profound or it may be viewed as simply cleverness disguising an inability to construct a clear plot and easy-to-understand characters.

Barthelme, Donald. *Sixty Stories*. 457p. NAL/Dutton, paper, (0-525-48453-1).

H. E. Bates
English. 1905–1974.

Bates is simply lovely. You read one Bates story and you'll ache to read more. He reached great heights in his writing and in his critical and popular reputations in the 1930s, when the short story in Britain was enjoying a renaissance. He was from Northamptonshire—a rural environment. His stories are derived from the land, his characters earthy and sensuous—the colors and smells and even the warmth or chill of the breeze playing over the countryside all pervade his stunning stories. Bates wrote with fine and moving lyricism, his sentences fraught with calm beauty. He often wrote about the steaminess that exists when a man and a woman, both secretly boiling with passion, find themselves in close proximity, or about the very human foibles of charming rustic characters. His "Uncle Silas" sequence is sheer delight—humorous, poignant, and positively endearing—with a vivid delineation of the title character. Admirers of D. H. Lawrence's short stories will enjoy those of Bates, for they share sensuousness in their writing.

Bates, H. E. *The Best of H. E. Bates.* 268p. Ayer (0-8369-3967-0).

Bates, H. E. *Uncle Silas.* 190p. Oxford, paper (0-19-281854-6).

Gina Berriault
American. 1926–1999.

Berriault's story "Zenobia" is an absolute tour de force. It has a gimmick, but the story is far from gimmicky. It is a smart, extremely clever, and amazingly original piece of writing, ostensibly addressed to famous writer Edith Wharton from one of her fictional creations, Zenobia, wife of the main character in Wharton's splendid and greatly evocative novella, *Ethan Frome.* In Berriault's story Zenobia denounces the life and plight Wharton gives her in her novella, and proffers a defense of the way she handled the relationship between Ethan and Mattie Silver, the young relative Zenobia had brought into the house to care for her. This story is a prime example of Berriault's phenomenol creativity. Every story she wrote is like no other story anyone has ever written. Until her recent death, she had been publishing for more than thirty years, and only toward the end of her life did she gain recognition as something more than a "writer's writer," which means that her talent is now appreciated by a wider reading public. The collection *Women in Their Beds* won both the PEN/Faulkner Award and the National Book Critics Circle Award. Her stories are generally about how individuals suffer in the world. Her prose style is exquisite without being mannered; she wrote with great irony, which correlates well with the economy with which she developed plot exposition and unfolded characterizations. She demonstrated an abiding understanding of peoples' emotional states. Her stories rarely offer tidy endings; she refused to "wrap things up" for readers, but left them to draw appropriate conclusions. She should not be missed. Another intriguing Berriault short story is "God and the Article Writer." What a psychological punch it delivers!

Berriault, Gina. *Women in Their Beds: New and Selected Stories.* 352p. Counterpoint, paper (1-887178-38-4).

29

MASTERS OF THE PAST

Ambrose Bierce
American. 1842–1914.

Bierce fought in the Civil War, became a journalist, and eventually disappeared in Mexico, never to be heard from again. He left behind a body of powerful short stories—stories about the Civil War, stories about horror, stories just to generate humor—yet always in a formal, controlled hand; always with tight, rich sentences; always with an eye to satire. A Bierce story has psychological twists and turns that challenge preconceived notions of reality. A darkness, a haunted feeling, pervades his work, as if, like Poe, he wrote from a corner of his heart where light rarely reached. "An Occurrence at Owl Creek Bridge" is about the execution of a soldier during the Civil War and features a startling ending. It is one of the most famous American short stories. Readers who firmly believe they prefer novels to short stories—that stories are too brief to really engage their interest—should read this story. It will jolt you out of your chair.

Bierce, Ambrose. *The Complete Short Stories of Ambrose Bierce.* 496p. University of Nebraska, paper (0-8032-6071-7).

Heinrich Böll
German. 1917–1985.

Böll figures as one of post-World War I Germany's most important writers, and, with Günter Grass, the most translated of all postwar German writers. Winner of the 1972 Nobel Prize, Böll earned a reputation as an extremely gifted writer. His gifts in the short-story form display themselves in full bloom in the brilliant story "Recollections of a Young King." At the age of thirteen, the crown prince of Capota succeeds to the throne when his father is assassinated by a "Rasac" ("Radical Sadists of Capota"); now the young king is free to choose not to do his homework: "on the whole I enjoyed being king because I could now deal differently with my tutor." Then a seemingly trivial incident necessitates his abdication, his kingdom ringing with "the whole terrible music of rebellion." He joins a circus and "get[s] to sniff the air of foreign lands." This story is, at once, a keen political satire, a fairy tale, and a social commentary. As in all of Böll's stories, the satire is muted by the author's air of amusement rather than disdain toward society. And this story demonstrates the trademark beauty of his style: simple and straightforward. He was an immaculate craftsman: he practiced, in every story, artful, lyrical simplicity. He built up his narratives with few details—but always the most telling and significant of details. And, in each story, he worked with few characters, to get his point across cleanly and assuredly.

Böll, Heinrich. *The Stories of Heinrich Böll.* 686p. Northwestern University, paper (0-8101-1207-8).

Jorge Luis Borges
Argentine. 1899–1986.

A seminal figure in Latin American literature, Borges is certainly one of the few great twentieth-century fiction writers who never wrote a novel; his high reputation rests upon his short stories alone. At the outset, the reader of Borges must surrender any predetermined ideas regarding what a story should be, for the man was a keen experimenter with form. A Borges story may take the guise of a biographical essay or even a book review. Fantasy was his workplace; he upset reality in order to expose life's disorder. Written in a highly polished and evocative style, his stories become vehicles not for depicting everyday events but rather for exploring intellectual concepts—creativity, the irrationality of the human mind, or the inability of humankind to accurately perceive truth or establish order in the world. "Tlon, Ugbar, Orbis Tertius," "The Library of Babel," "The South," and "Death and the Compass" are famous stories—cerebral inventions that demand more than one reading.

Borges, Jorge Luis. *Collected Fictions.* 565p. Viking (0-670-84970-7); Penguin, paper (0-14-028680-2).

Elizabeth Bowen
Anglo-Irish. 1899–1973.

The autobiographical *Bowen's Court* (1942) is a magnificent history of the author's family, English-descent landowners in Ireland's County Cork. Bowen knew two worlds—England and the Ireland of the Anglo-Irish gentry—and she wrote about both in her stories. Her style is the most deciding factor in enjoying Bowen. Some perceive her sentences as too rich, too convoluted for easy digestion; others find them readily embraceable, even exhilarating. Beyond that, a Bowen story is always furnished with roomfuls of luxurious detail. "Summer Night," for instance, about a woman driving through a lovely, warm evening to rendezvous with her lover, offers beautiful, scene-setting description that begs to be reread and read aloud. Also notable are "The Demon Lover," an impeccably conceived ghost story set in London during the blitz of World War II, and the intriguing "Happy Autumn Fields," with its unusual time shifts back and forth between World War II London and Victorian Ireland. Male-female relations and childhood were Bowen's forte. She is for sophisticated fiction readers already convinced of the virtues of the short-story form.

Bowen, Elizabeth. *The Collected Stories of Elizabeth Bowen.* 784p.
   Ecco, paper (0-88001-493-8).

Paul Bowles
American. 1910–1999.

To think of Paul Bowles is to think of Morocco. This New York City-born writer lived a great portion of his life in that North African country, whose distinctions of atmosphere and custom and—perhaps most importantly—mysteriousness imbue his luscious novels and stories. Regretably, Bowles is most often described as a "writer's writer"—i.e., recognized as top-notch by peers but lacking widespread appreciation from the general reading public. Despite this limited reputation, Bowles is marvelous. In writing of Morocco and another of his favorite locales, Mexico, he paid particular attention to the clash of alien and native cultures—specifically, what foreigners perceive and what they are incapable of perceiving about indigenous habits and attitudes, and vice versa. There is often a dreamy unreality about a Bowles story, as if narrated by Scheherezade; but quickly the dream can turn into a nightmare, with dreadful violence or acute madness or, at the very least, unbelievable cruelty. His style is beautifully unpretentious and graceful in its simultaneous brevity and resonance. "The Delicate Prey" is an extremely unforgettable impression of Bowles' Morocco.

Bowles, Paul. *Collected Stories 1939–1976.* 417p. Black Sparrow,
    paper (0-87685-396-3).

Kay Boyle
American. 1903–1992.

Featuring a wide range of settings—reflective of the fact that much
of the author's life was spent abroad—Boyle's stories feature both
American and European characters, many of whom have been affected
by the hostilities of World War II and its difficult aftermath. Boyle
was always involved in political and social activism. Her stories are
told in traditional narrative form and revolve around value conflicts,
either personal ones—who to love, who to hate, and why—or cultural ones between opposing groups: Jewish and Gentile, white and
black, different nationalities. The slices of life offered here are
smoothly cut, resulting in subtle but deep character revelations. "The
Rest Cure" is a very forceful piece of writing about an invalid writer.
(Knowing the dying D. H. Lawrence to be the protagonist reveals the
story's special poignancy.) And "The White Horses of Vienna" is very
evocatively grounded in the political unrest of 1934 Austria.

Boyle, Kay. *Fifty Stories.* 648p. New Directions, paper
    (0-8112-1206-8).

Harold Brodkey
American. 1930–1996.

Despite the fact that his stories were published in the *New Yorker* and
Esquire, only the most discriminating of serious fiction readers knew
Brodkey's name. And yet his work is a veritable feast. Some of his stories
stand firmly in the genre's traditional vein: trim narratives building
toward an epiphanous moment in one character's life. Others, often
about the sex act, ramble more in the manner of stream-of-con-
sciousness. Still others are gusts of memory, mostly about childhood,
recalled by a first-person narrator. All of his stories flow with exquisite
but unselfconscious language, roll with beautifully yet carefully
wrought images. In all, Brodkey's stories are both challenging and
thrilling—stellar examples of the variety of expressiveness that a

master of the short story can achieve. "The Bullies" presents a porch dialogue between two women friends, their conversation witnessed by one woman's young son. We are privy to both what these women say and what they *don't* say as they verbally test and retest the mutual waters surrounding their friendship.

Brodkey, Harold. *The World Is the Home of Love and Death.* 312p. Holt/Metropolitan (0-8050-5513-4).

Erskine Caldwell
American. 1903–1987.

The controversial author of the novels *Tobacco Road* (1932) and *God's Little Acre* (1933) has always borne a reputation for reveling in the seamy underside of poor southern life. Caldwell often wrote about the coarse relationship between poor rural black and white folks in the South in the early and middle parts of this century. He dealt with the sordid, baser aspects of human nature, eschewing well-roundedness in his characters in order to turn the reader's scrutiny toward their grotesque sides. Yet his depictions are ironically impersonal and even humorous—there is no groaning or sweating over the plight of these pathetic people. Caldwell's style is simple yet exact, and despite his notoriety for naughty humor, he was a dedicated writer, an even finer practitioner of the short story than the novel. "Candy-Man Beechum" is a frequently anthologized story about a black mule skinner going into town on a Saturday night to see his girl.

Caldwell, Erskine. *The Stories of Erskine Caldwell.* 664p. University of Georgia, paper (0-8203-1994-6).

Karol Capek
Czech. 1890–1938.

Tales from Two Pockets is a delightful collection of short stories. The first tale is called "Dr. Mejzlik's Case"; it sets the tone for all the stories that follow. An inexperienced police detective has apprehended a safecracker, but his success in solving the crime is discomfiting to him. The whole police force is saying "that Mejzlik, he's got a real flair; that young fellow with the glasses is going to go places with his talents as a detective." But the detective is reacting unfavorably to the praise: he believes he solved the safecracking case only by chance and fears that on the next case everyone will be watching him to see his fine investigative methods at play again. Characteristics of the collection as a whole are established in this first story: Capek's use of clear language, the charm of his characters, and the fact that each story deals in some fashion with a mystery—that these are basically detective stories, although they do not always include a real crime or the solution to one. The characters appearing in these stories are ordinary people caught up in extraordinary circumstances. Capek was a leading Czech writer of the 1920s and 1930s; in his prime, in fact, he was one of the world's greatest writers and the most internationally recognized Czech writer of his day. He also wrote novels, plays, and a newspaper column; his plays appeared on Broadway soon after their premieres on the Prague stage. But *Tales from Two Pockets* has proven to be his most admired book at home and abroad, and reading just a couple stories from it will show readers why.

Capek, Karol. *Tales from Two Pockets*. 365p. Catbird, paper (0-945774-25-7).

Angela Carter
British. 1940–1992.

British by birth, Carter was a cosmopolite by inclination. She died early, from cancer, cutting her career far too short: "in mid-sentence, as it were," as friend and fellow writer Salmon Rushdie has said. She had an incredible imagination; she is recognized as one of Britain's most original writers. Author of several novels, Carter nonetheless is better known for her short stories, which, fortunately, have been brought together in one volume. Her stories were fabulous, in both senses of the word—fablelike and wonderful. She mixed folklore with fairy tale and came up with her own variations, often with feminist revisions. Despite many stories that are in a realistic vein, Carter was most at home in evoking the world of fable and fantasy, with appropriate atmospheres of castles, dark nights, and howling wolves. She was fascinated by violence and used sexual motivation as a story springboard; her interest in these themes extended into the realms of incest, sadism, and sexual deviation. She wrote in a gently poetic style: her use of luxuriant language worked magnificently in conveying strong visual images. The long story "The Bloody Chamber" is probably her masterpiece. A seventeen-year-old girl has just married a much older man, the richest in France, and on their wedding night she travels with him to his castle. With distinct gothic overtones, the young bride's first-person narrative relates her discovery that her husband is a bluebeard.

Carter, Angela. *Burning Your Boats: The Collected Short Stories.* 480p. Penguin, paper (0-14-025528-1).

Raymond Carver
American. 1938–1988.

Until his untimely death, Carver was the fountainhead of the minimalist school of short-story writing that in Carver's prime, the 1980s, was quite the literary fashion. He told nothing more than what the reader absolutely needed to know about a character or a situation, letting a significant detail here and there denote and connote the present conditions and circumstances. Carver dwelt on the commonplace: the small but personally consequential bad turn of fortune in ordinary lower- and middle-class lives. A flat style, forgotten people, a seemingly trivial crisis—these are the ingredients of a Carver tale. "Careful" is a good example of why some people say, "It's not what Carver put in a story so much as it was what he left out"; why some people feel that a Carver story is so wonderfully ambiguous it lends itself to all kinds of meaning and significance, resonating with a universal human experience. But this tale also exemplifies why other people think Carver fell flat; an annoyingly simplistic, monotonous tone; characters too boring to care about; not a flash of brilliance in the whole narrative, only a depressing whine, like listening to a tedious next-door neighbor going on about his troubles. Read him and judge for yourself.

Carver, Raymond. *Cathedral.* 227p. Random/Vintage, paper (0-679-72369-2).

Willa Cather

American. 1873–1947.

Virginia-born but Nebraska-raised, Cather, through her Great Plains frontier experiences, filtered her courage-oriented sensibilities to produce warm-blooded yet dignified fiction. On one hand, she can be read for style alone. Elegant simplicity and perfect lucidity distinguish her prose. But the substance of her tales also touches the reader deeply. Cather wrote about hard lives, noble lives. Specifically, her work often deals with the conflicts faced in society by individuals of artistic sensitivity. Her novels are among the best written by an American in the twentieth century; these masterpieces include *My Ántonia, The Professor's House,* and *The Lost Lady.* (Her novel *One of Ours* won the 1923 Pulitzer Prize but ranks lower than the three mentioned masterpieces in most critics' eyes.) As much as her stories dwell in the shadows of these classics, they should not be overlooked. All of Cather's best traits appear in her stories in concentration. "Paul's Case," her most famous story, beautifully demonstrates her abiding theme of artistic sensitivity facing an insensitive world. (In fact, it is subtitled "A Study in Temperament.") Paul is a dreamy youth crushed to death by conformity.

Cather, Willa. *Collected Stories.* 493p. Random/Vintage
    (0-679-73648-4).

John Cheever

American. 1912–1982.

Cheever was a chronicler of middle-class suburban America. In such stories as "Youth and Beauty!" "The Swimmer," and "The Trouble of Marcie Flint," he used stiletto-sharp humor to expose the truth about suburbia's shady streets, backyard swimming pools, and that great battleground, the bedroom. Cheever knew instinctively the details of his characters' lives: what they said and ate and drank, how they were employed, and who they pretended to be and feared they actually were. He wrote with splendid eloquence—a gold mine for readers who thrill over an extensive vocabulary, intriguing syntax, and lush description, ideas, and authorial commentary. Yet his stories don't

seem overblown at all. Instead, they seem quite natural, as if someone very well spoken were relating the stories orally. It is amazingly
easy to lose oneself in a Cheever story—and then to want to keep
reading them one right after the other. His novel *The Wapshot
Chronicles* won the 1958 National Book Award and the *Stories of John
Cheever* won both the National Book Critics Circle Award and the
Pulitzer Prize for 1978.

Cheever, John. *The Stories of John Cheever.* 693p. Knopf
(0-394-50087-3); Ballantine, paper (0-345-33567-8).

Anton Chekhov
Russian. 1860–1904.

The supreme master—czar, perhaps?—of implication and sugges-
tion, of telling stories by offering a nugget of information here and
briefly sketching in a nuance there. Because of the sheer significance
of each of these selective details—rather than their cumulative
impact—the reader comes to a quiet realization of just exactly what
a character is all about. Chekhov's stories are gentle, humorous, and
poignant; but that doesn't mean they are insubstantial. They spring
forth and crackle with real life, with as much vitality in the complex
twentieth century as they did in the less-hurried nineteenth.
Chekhov drew his material from all walks of Russian life—peasantry
and aristocracy, men and women, military and bureaucracy. No one
who is interested in short stories, especially in writing a short story,
should miss "The Lady with the Pet Dog" or "Gooseberries." These
are, like nearly every story he wrote, masterpieces of sensitive rendering of human nature, of sympathetic views of the narrownesses of
human thought and behavior.

Chekhov, Anton. *The Russian Master and Other Stories.* 233p.
Oxford, paper (0-19-281680-2).

Kate Chopin
American. 1851–1904.

Kate Chopin is an interesting literary case. A member of a socially
prominent family in St. Louis, she married a Louisiana cotton broker

and plantation owner. Left a widow early, she returned to St. Louis, and there began a writing career. Her novel *The Awakening* was published in 1899. Its frank sensuality was roundly vilified for immorality, and Chopin's literary reputation went into a tailspin. But recently this splendid novel has been recognized as a masterpiece and is being taught in the college classroom. A readership is growing for her short stories as well. They are set in the Louisiana Chopin came to know as a married woman, among the Creoles and Cajuns with whom she was familiar. She focused particularly on women's wants and needs in marriage, treating love and sexuality with psychological incisiveness and abiding sensuality, but also with moral objectivity. Chopin's approach was realistic, her sentences economically rendered, with each word chosen for its opalescence. The brief "Desirée's Baby" is a staggering story about racial mixing.

Chopin, Kate. *The Awakening and Selected Stories.* 286p. Penguin, paper (0-14039022-7).

Colette
French. 1876–1954.

Colette is one of the giants of twentieth-century French literature as well as one of the best loved; France marked the occasion of her death with a state funeral. She was an original: she wrote her own way and no one else's. Her writing is steeped in autobiography; in fact, she appears as a character in many of her stories. She drew heavily from her personal experiences: her country childhood in Burgundy, her unhappy first marriage to a man who locked her in her room and forced her to write works he published under his own name, and her years on the stage. Don't make the grave mistake of passing Colette off as a woman's magazine-type fiction writer without reading her for yourself. She is renowned for two trademarks: her exquisitely delicate prose style and her sensuality (in other words, her inhabitation of the world of the senses, where the tastes, textures, and aromas of the physical world are matched with the urges of the heart and the flesh). Her lyrical descriptions of nature are to be savored. She exhibits great sensitivity to and understanding of childhood, but all her psychological observations, about adults as well as children, are as keen as razors. The brief story "April" shows the qualities of Colette in sharp focus. Two teenagers, boyfriend and girlfriend, join a group of friends for a bicycle day-trip. Their love for each other is tenderly wrought, as we would expect from the sensitive Colette. "Whenever he felt happy, he appealed, with words and gestures, to Vinca. She tilted back her head to gaze up at the tree and her blue eyes filled with splendor. Nothing more was needed for them to feel bound to each other and withdrawn into that secret place where their tenderness regained its strength and self-awareness." And, of course, Colette is careful to paint a delicate picture of nature as it provides a setting for these young peoples' excursion out into it. But the boy and the girl stumble upon a couple just having made love, and he wants to shield her from the sight and its meaning. An achingly beautiful story of young love.

Colette. *The Collected Stories of Colette*. 605p. Penguin, paper (0-14-018318-3).

Joseph Conrad
Polish-born, naturalized British, 1857–1924

Conrad went to sea as a teenager, and his experiences gave him much to write about. (Amazingly, English was an acquired language.) His long tales are powerful and exciting portraits of men facing adversity—nature's brutal elements or man's inhumanity to man—and what it takes to overcome it. Conjuring up the right atmosphere was crucial to Conrad's vision. What's in the air often brings out what's in the character. Nuance of expression was not his style. Instead, he created big, bold images, with every sentence carrying great pictorial weight. A Conrad story is quite vivid, then. The reader is virtually sucked into the scene depicted in "Heart of Darkness"—up the Congo River, where the protagonist has discovered, and is overcome by, humanity's hidden carnivorous nature.

Conrad, Joseph. *Heart of Darkness and Other Tales*. 298p. Oxford University, paper (0-19283373-1).

A. E. Coppard
English. 1878–1957.

Coppard was self-taught in literature and didn't publish until later than most fiction writers. He never wrote a novel; his reputation rests entirely on his stories. And his stories are sufficiently solid to support an entire literary reputation. They serve as guide to the English countryside, introducing to the reader a bevy of quietly noble folk. There is a fablelike—a folkloric—simple dignity to his stories. He strikes the reader as both ingenuous and a genius. On the surface, Coppard's sentences seem to be artlessly straightforward, but then it becomes clear that each phrase has been cut like an expensive gem, with perfect facets reflecting sheer poetic beauty. Coppard is best read slowly, in order to feel his vigor, his power, and his exquisite sensitivity. "The Field of Mustard" is an exemplary tale. It is about two women out gathering kindling; in the process they contrast the bleakness of the world as it is with the idyllic way they'd like the world to be.

Coppard, A. E. *The Collected Tales of A. E. Coppard.* 532p. Ayer (0-405-08119-7).

Julio Cortázar
Argentine. 1914–1984.

Born in Brussels of Argentine parents, Cortázar later became a French citizen, but he is definitely identified as a Latin American writer. Like his compatriot Borges, Cortázar is clever but not easy to embrace. Nonetheless, he is a wonderful challenge, offering fantastic stories based on some mysterious force that insinuates itself into and then manipulates peoples' lives, stories brimming with word play, in-jokes, and such cerebral concerns as the meanings of existence and reality. The very political "Apocalypse at Solentiname" serves as a good example of a typical Cortázar story. This discomfiting—no, shocking—narrative takes the form of a testimony of a famous Latin American writer (parallels to Cortázar himself are strong) recounting a trip to Central America, where he photographed some folk-style paintings he discovered on the island of Solentiname off the coast of Nicaragua. Later, back in Paris, he has the photos developed into slides; but when he sits down to view them, what he sees on the screen are not images of the delightful paintings he loved so much, but horrible scenes of human massacre.

Cortázar, Julio. *Blow-Up and Other Stories.* 277p. Random/Vintage, paper (0-394-72881-5).

Stephen Crane
American. 1871–1900.

"None of them knew the color of the sky." That's the opening line of Crane's famous story about shipwreck, "The Open Boat." Who could possibly resist, after reading that brief but potent sentence, wanting to find out who these people are and why they aren't noticing the sky above them. Crane led an adventurous life, one that was not entirely respectable. Critics still argue whether he was a realist, a naturalist, or an impressionist. That debate is specious, however. Simply relish Crane's use of varied settings: urban centers, the West, the locales he encountered as a war correspondent. Crane dealt with big moral and life-and-death issues, and no matter how his technique is categorized, he remains a clear, precise, indelible, even lovely writer. "The Blue Hotel," which concerns the contentious guests at a hotel in frontier Nebraska during a raging blizzard, and "The Bride Comes to Yellow Sky," which takes place at a time when the Old West is dying out, form, with "The Open Boat," a trio of his most frequently anthologized, and best, stories.

Crane, Stephen. *The Great Short Works of Stephen Crane.* 384p. HarperCollins, paper (0-060-83032-8).

Walter de la Mare
English. 1873–1956.

De la Mare wrote in a grand, bold, decorated, unrestrained style, not designed for carefree reading. His tales of horror, fantasy, and the supernatural feature plots built on involved frameworks, which require patience in absorbing them one step at a time. Nevertheless, they're marvelous works. Taking a typical English setting, in town or country—a house, a garden, a railway station—de la Mare injects some kind of insidious evil or unnaturalness. A sense of foreboding is followed by increased suspense—and the reader remains haunted long after the story has been finished. "The House" is a good example of the author's chilling manner. A man who knows he's dying tours his own domicile for the very last time.

De la Mare, Walter. *Best Stories of Walter de la Mare*. 397p. Faber and Faber, paper (0-571-13076-3).

Isak Dinesen
Danish. 1885–1962.

Isak Dinesen was the pseudonym of Karen Blixen, whose life was brought to widespread public attention with the 1985 movie *Out of Africa,* starring Meryl Streep and Robert Redford. Blixen married a distant cousin, a Swedish baron, and in 1913 they went to East Africa to found a coffee plantation. It was not an uncomplicated venture; divorced, having left the plantation forever, Blixen returned home to Denmark and began writing for financial reasons. Her stories are fables and fairy tales—big, unabashed expositions on the travails of kings, queens, nobles, and fashionable society in love and in lust or embroiled in adventures or calamities caused by nature or the supernatural. The settings are the historical past, with lots of threatening atmosphere and plenty of costumes and written in a baroque style. But beneath the romantic facades there lurks a very precise, sensitive, and delicate understanding of the nuances of character. Finely carved and shaded personalities exist behind the gothic trappings of a Dinesen story. A prime example is "The Deluge at Norderney," a long involved tale concerning a storm in 1835, which wreaks havoc on the lives of certain individuals at a Danish resort. It's a wonderful psychological fathoming.

Dinesen, Isak. *Seven Gothic Tales*. 420p. Random/Vintage, paper (0-679-73641-5).

Andre Dubus
American. 1936–1999.

For many years, Dubus was regarded as an up-and-coming short story writer, then when he'd finally arrived critically, popularly, and commercially, he died. In many of his stories, Dubus writes about love and marriage, the problems inherent in trying to keep one, if not both, alive. Other tales are based on his personal military experiences—in the Marines—and deal with the physical strain and the emotional distress of such a disciplined life. Dubus is not an artsy writer; there is an unembellished yet eloquent ordinariness about his style. He builds a narrative in a leisurely manner, making it easy to fall into his rhythms, to see where he is going with a character. There may be a bit too much descriptive detail in many of the stories—but that is quibbling. Dubus definitely understood the art of the short story, and his work is accessible to all readers. "Miranda over the Valley" is one of his finest examinations of relationships.

Dubus, Andre. *Selected Stories*. 480p. Random/Vintage, paper (0-679-76730-4).

William Faulkner
American. 1897–1962.

Faulkner created one of literature's most fully realized, enduring worlds: his fictional Mississippi county of Yoknapatawpha. You can visit the fictional Yoknapatawpha County by way of his novels, of course, but they are awfully complicated, in terms of both plot and sentence structure. But his stories offer a less-circuitous itinerary, which is to say that his notoriously abstruse plots and long, involved sentences are less full-blown and thus less an obstruction to appreciating his version of Mississippi and its diverse society. Faulkner was fascinated with the shift from Old South to New, with the degeneration of genteel families, with human nature's propensity for perversion, and with the absurdity in the lives of eccentric people. The very accessible "Dry September" gives clear indication of the depth of his passionate—even obsessive—feeling for the South. And "A Rose for Emily" is a splendidly gothic tale concerning an eccentric woman who becomes increasingly reclusive; on her death the townspeople discover her horrible secret. Faulkner won the Nobel Prize in 1954, the Pulitzer Prize in 1955 (for *A Fable)* and again in 1963 (for *The Reivers)*, and a National Book Award in 1951 for his *Collected Stories.*

Faulkner, William. *Collected Stories of William Faulkner.* 900p. Random/Vintage, paper (0-679-76403-8).

Dorothy Canfield Fisher
American. 1879–1950.

Fisher was one of the most successful writers, artistically and commercially, during the first half of the twentieth century. She was prolific: the author of more than forty books, including novels and nonfiction titles as well as short-story collections. Her heyday was the 1920s through the 1940s, but she is little read these days; she has been, in fact, pretty much forgotten. That is not as it should be, though, for her stories, in particular, continue to speak to readers in the present day. The compactness of the short-story form suited her talents and voice best. Her stories reflect her long involvement in social causes; their placid surfaces, achieved by a consummately limpid style, do not blunt their effectiveness as honest explorations of emotional provinces. Racial and social questions are treated with compassion and a clear-sighted view of less-than-noble traits in humanity. Also, her cosmopolitanism is reflected in her stories, offering great breadth and range in terms of settings and types of characters across gender, economic, and national boundaries (for instance, some are set in southeast France during World War I). Fisher was an expert at tight plot development, the ways of spoken language, and recognizing the significant detail. "The Bedquilt," set in New England, is the poignant story of Aunt Mehetabel, an "old maid" treated with disregard by her family and who has "never for a moment known the pleasure of being important to anyone." Then she makes a quilt by a design of her own creation, which earns first prize at the country fair, and with that she has achieved her place in life.

Fisher, Dorothy Canfield. *The Bedquilt and Other Stories.* 256p. University of Missouri, paper (0-8262-1035-X).

Rudolph Fisher
American. 1902–1967.

Fisher was a stellar contributor to the Harlem Renaissance, the black cultural movement centered in Harlem in the 1920s. He is little read today, unfortunately, but his short stories should prove fascinating to anyone interested in the form or in black culture in the interwar period. Fisher was a practicing physician and a writer simultaneously, but his stories are definitely not the product of a Sunday dabbler. The rhythmic cadences of his style and his stance toward his race—at once humorous, sensitive, and prideful but not defensive—work together to make these pieces about lives of ordinary folks in Harlem both eminently artful and exceptionally inviting. Fisher wrote of black people recently arrived in Harlem and getting used to its streets and attitudes, and he wrote of well-worn Harlemites whose bodies and souls suffered no less than that of the newcomers. "John Archer's Nose," a detective story, is particularly appealing.

Fisher, Rudolph. *The City of Refuge: The Collected Stories of Rudolph Fisher.* 240p. University of Missouri, paper (0-8262-0786-3).

F. Scott Fitzgerald
American. 1896–1940.

"Let me tell you about the very rich. They are different from you and me," says Fitzgerald in his story "The Rich Boy." In effect a social historian of the Jazz Age, Fitzgerald became legendary for living fast, for writing about the moneyed class, for burning out quickly. At least one of his novels, *The Great Gatsby,* will remain forever in the canon of twentieth-century American classics. It is an immaculate piece of writing. His stories are less so, however. Many of them were cranked out for quick consumer-magazine publication, mainly to put money into his pocket. But all of them are still worth reading as greatly entertaining jaunts back to a time that continues to hold fascination. The lives of men and women in and out of sync with each other preoccupied Fitzgerald, and he served up these little dramas with a glib tone and ingratiatingly clever style. "May Day" and "The Diamond as Big as the Ritz" are more profound than most of his stories.

Fitzgerald, F. Scott. *The Short Stories of F. Scott Fitzgerald*. 512p.
    Scribner, paper (0-684-80445-X).

Gustave Flaubert
French. 1821–1880.

Flaubert is celebrated for his realism—his mastery at depicting ordinary people and their normal experiences as well as their very realistic descriptions of exotic settings. He is also acclaimed for his perfection of style: careful attention was paid to every sentence he wrote.
Flaubert wrote about love, faith, and sensuousness, painting rich verbal pictures that impart to the reader just how things looked, felt to
the touch, or sounded and smelled. His most admired short story is
"The Simple Heart." To purists who insist a short story should entail
only an isolated moment, this piece will seem to be a condensed
novel, with too many episodes over too long a time frame to qualify
as a "real" short story. Nevertheless, it remains a moving portrayal of
the life of the good maidservant, Felicite.

Flaubert, Gustave. *Three Tales*. 124p. Penguin, paper (0-14-044106-9)

Mary E. Wilkins Freeman
American. 1852–1930.

Freeman is labeled a "local colorist," but that shouldn't imply that
her New England-based stories are harmless, humorous little sketches
rendered in the fewest and faintest of brushstrokes, with appeal limited to people familiar with the area. The truth of the matter is that
Freeman's stories transcend both the time in which they take place—
the late nineteenth century—and their locale to speak to readers of
today. She wrote about granite-hard New England women of the
countryside and small towns, characters of resistance and resilience
in the face of hard climate, hard soil, hard men. Freeman realistically
sketched the interiors of these women's lives, carefully insinuating a
comprehension of their strengths of will. All of this is delivered in a
crystalline style. In "The Revolt of 'Mother,'" Mother is upset with
Father for building another barn when what they really need is a big-
ger house. So she moves the family into the newly completed barn
while he's away.

Freeman, Mary E. Wilkins. *A Mary Wilkins Freeman Reader.* 450p.
 University of Nebraska, paper (0-8032-6894-7).

Caroline Gordon
American. 1895–1981.

Gordon and her husband, poet Allen Tate, were participants in the
so-called Southern Renaissance—the rise to superior status of a
number of southern U.S. writers in the first half of this century.
Gordon, born in Kentucky, wrote about the land and what it produced, and about the families who lived on it and their ties to each
other. She was obsessively southern, and her writing is abidingly
concerned with the order and dignity of the South's agrarian past and
the social confusion she saw in its industrial present. Gordon was a
psychological writer, an analyzer of relationships and their causa-
tions, conditions, consequences. She maintained a poised, unobtrusive use of history—the Civil War, particularly—in some of her stories,
such as "Hear the Nightingale Sing." The fact that they are set in the
past is important to their premise, not because Gordon was contriv-
ing an artificial stage on which to conduct a costume drama. "Old
Red," Gordon's most famous story, shows her to be a dexterous
painter of detail. It features a protagonist Gordon uses in other fictional works, Professor Aleck Maury, who loves to fish.

Gordon, Caroline. *The Collected Stories of Caroline Gordon.* 368p.
 J. S. Sanders, paper (1-879-94144-9).

Graham Greene
English. 1904–1991.

The highly respected, avidly read English novelist wrote superb short
stories throughout his long career. An ardent traveler, Greene set stories
in all kinds of faraway places, from Africa to Mexico. Like his longer
works, his stories deal, essentially, with the darker sides of religion
and love, but leavened with humor and compassion. They often are
comedies dealing with sexual situations. And he is superb at conjuring atmospheric effects. There is not an extraneous utterance,
description, or incident in Greene's taut narratives. His characters
range widely through quirky sorts of people—each one wonderfully

involving, clearly defined, well shaded, completely original. "The Basement Room" is one of his most remarkable short works, revealing Greene's psychological astuteness. When a little boy is left home in London in the care of the family butler and the housekeeper, his life is traumatized forever. It was filmed in 1948 as *The Fallen Idol*.

Greene, Graham. *Collected Short Stories*. 400p. Penguin, paper (0-14-018612-3).

Nathaniel Hawthorne
American. 1804–1864.

Born in the old town of Salem, Massachusetts, the highly intelligent Hawthorne mined the historical past for material and delved into the supernatural for powerful effect. His very psychological stories deal with good and evil; he probes moral issues and reports his findings in terms of black and white, with very little gray shading. Nonetheless, Hawthorne remains one of the most compelling of early American contributors to the story genre. He relied heavily on the use of symbol and allegory; the symbols are organic to the stories and thus work without actually having to be recognized as such by the reader; ignoring the allegorical levels simply means they can still be enjoyed for their rich but very controlled language and their eerie drama. "Ethan Brand" and "Rappaccini's Daughter" are prime examples of Hawthorne's multilevel expression. The first concerns a lime burner tending his fire with his son, when they are approached by a man, a former lime burner who now devotes his life to searching for the "unpardonable sin." In the second story, we see a young Italian student whose lodgings overlook a spectacular garden belonging to Dr. Rappaccini, whose scientific experiments involve his own daughter, Beatrice.

Hawthorne, Nathaniel. *Tales and Sketches*. 1,493p. Library of America (0-940450-03-8).

Ernest Hemingway
American. 1899–1961.

Clean, simple sentences. Hemingway is famous for them. And for writing about male bravado in the face of adversity. The truth of the matter is, anyone interested in learning the fundamentals of expressive writing would do well to study each and every sentence in Hemingway's short stories. He's had imitators, but none have come close to his sheer eloquence. As far as his obsession with hairy-chested men and their courage under pressure—well, that can pose a slight irritation to the reader initially, but it is never a permanent impediment to the enjoyment of his writing. His stories are, without a doubt, arresting in their abrupt accuracy of speech and manner and psychology; and underneath his seemingly chauvinistic stances, Hemingway could show sensitivity to insecurities. Sports activities, the out-of-doors, violent death, war: these were Hemingway's preoccupations. Stories such as "Big Two-Hearted River," which features Hemingway's recurrent character, Nick Adams, in an adventure of camping and fishing, and "The Killers," in which Nick Adams is inadvertently caught up in gangland affairs, show how well he knew these physical/emotional terrains. Hemingway won the 1954 Nobel Prize and, for *The Old Man and the Sea,* the 1953 Pulitzer Prize.

Hemingway, Ernest. *The Complete Short Stories of Ernest Hemingway.* 672p. Scribner, paper (0-684-84332-3).

O. Henry
American. 1862–1910.

O. Henry, pseudonym of William Sydney Porter, was the supreme practitioner of the trick ending, the ironic twist which, rather than putting a nice cap on the story, slaps the reader in the face with a complete surprise. Not a particularly admirable device, it can too often hide slipshod narrative development—which in O. Henry's case it often did. Nevertheless, O. Henry greatly popularized the short story, giving it strength in the public's mind as something perfectly suited to satisfying the need to be entertained. His knowledge of real people—whether those found in New York or out West or in Latin America—was thorough and sensitive, and there's an authenticity to his writing that is to be admired. "The Gift of the Magi" shows the trick ending at work, but the story leaves you moved as well. It is one of the first short stories young readers encounter, a poignant piece about a poor young couple's mutual sacrifices to buy each other a Christmas present.

Henry, O. *Selected Stories*. 384p. Penguin, paper (0-14-018688-3).

E. T. A. Hoffmann
German. 1776–1822.

Hoffmann was part of the German branch of the Romantic movement, which swept European literature and art in the eighteenth and nineteenth centuries. Adherents believed in the essential goodness of humankind and in the primacy of nature and of the senses over civilization and reason. Romanticism led Hoffmann, along with many other practitioners, inside himself—to explore, in his works, dreams and fantasy (fairy tales, tales of the macabre). Thus, he wrote of aberrant individuals, strange situations, supernatural conditions. His characters might be artists outside mainstream society, or even split personalities. Hoffmann's diction is old-fashioned in its formality, though his insights into haunted corners of the mind are as immaculately on target as the day they were written. "Mademoiselle de Scuderi," long but fast moving, is a detective story set in Paris during the reign of Louis XIV, centering on a robbery-and-murder spree that has the city terrorized. Hoffmann's influence on Edgar Allan Poe is well in evidence in this tale.

Hoffmann, E. T. A. *The Tales of Hoffmann*. 411p. Penguin, paper (0-14-044392-4).

Langston Hughes
American. 1902–1967.

Hughes was one of the most significant twentieth-century black writers. In addition to short stories, he was also accomplished in the novel, drama, poetry, and autobiography. He wrote of black people in Harlem, in farming regions, in Florida, all over the country—and focused on the raw edge of black-and-white relations. Hughes distilled the various bruisings involved in the black experience in this country, but his point of view isolated black pride as well. He wrote not with vitriol but in the honest pursuit of truth. Many of Hughes's stories feature the character Jesse B.

Semple, called Simple, a street-wise Harlemite brimming with tales and homespun philosophy. The obvious humor aside, the Simple stories are forceful depictions of Harlem life and, by representation, the universal black experience. "Little Dog" is not a Simple story, but one in a serious vein concerning a white woman who obtains a dog and has the black janitor get meat for it every day. In time, it is the janitor, not the dog, the woman longs to see when she gets home from work. A disturbing situation, and a disturbing story.

Hughes, Langston. *The Ways of White Folks.* 256p. Random/ Vintage, paper (0-679-72817-1).

Zora Neale Hurston
American. 1903–1960.

Hurston was a major contributor to the Harlem Renaissance arts movement of the 1920s and 1930s, but her popularity declined in the 1940s and 1950s and she died in relative obscurity. A Hurston revival occurred in the 1970s, spearheaded by writer Alice Walker, and now Hurston's reputation is securely high again and her works are vital members of the American literary canon. She was born in the all-black town of Eatonville, Florida, near Orlando. She experienced a happy early childhood free of poverty and racism and grew to possess a fiercely independent temperament. Her novels are back in public notice, even more popular now than when they were first published, particularly her acknowledged masterpiece, *Their Eyes Were Watching God* (1937), which is currently taught in classrooms. Hurston was also an important collector of black folklore, and her fiction is largely based in black folk tradition and written in black folk idiom. Her short stories generally were written before her novels and they introduce many of the themes she would later develop in her longer works; these include love, jealousy, betrayal, guilt, death, superstition, the triumph of love over evil and of the powerless over the powerful. Most of her stories are set in her native Florida. "The Gilded Six-Bits" is a favorite story of Hurston's readers, frequently anthologized. Joe and Missie May's marriage nearly founders on the rocks of infidelity, but an eventual reconciliation is not impossible. Many of Hurston's thematic concerns are aired in this moving story.

Hurston, Zora Neale. *The Complete Stories.* 336p. HarperPerennial, paper (0-06-092171-4).

Washington Irving
American. 1783–1859.

Irving was the first writer in the new American nation to gain stature abroad. Most of his work is not all that exciting these days, with the exception of two stories from *The Sketch Book of Geoffrey Crayon, Gent.*—"Rip Van Winkle," who, of course, fell asleep for twenty years and awakened as an old man; and "The Legend of Sleepy Hollow," the famous tale of schoolmaster Ichabod Crane and the headless horseman. These two stories should be read by everyone; they retain great charm. Irving wrote them in a style that is graceful, exacting, colorful. For example, the description of Ichabod Crane: "He was tall, but exceedingly lank, with narrow shoulders, long arms and legs, hands that dangled a mile out of his sleeves, feet that might have served for shovels, and his whole frame most loosely hung together. His head was small, and flat at top, with huge ears, large green glassy eyes, and a long snipe nose, so that it looked like a weathercock, perched upon his spindle neck, to tell which way the wind blew. To see him striding along the profile of a hill on a windy day, with his clothes bagging and fluttering about him, one might have mistaken him for the genius of famine descending upon the earth, or some scarecrow eloped from a cornfield."

Irving, Washington. *Sketch Book.* 389p. NAL/Dutton, paper (0-451-52495-0).

Shirley Jackson
American. 1919–1965.

Most readers first encounter Jackson in high-school English, assigned to read her most famous story, "The Lottery," which is one of the most widely anthologized American short stories. It stunned readers upon its first publication in the June 26, 1948, issue of the *New Yorker*, and it has been making readers gasp with shock ever since. On a summer morning, the residents of a small New England town gather for the annual lottery. Underlying the festive atmosphere is an increasing sense of nervousness and tension. And what a face-slapping denouement: the "winner" of the lottery is stoned to death, the latest scapegoat to ward off evils that might beset the community. The odd twist of circumstance in an everyday setting is a common storytelling technique of Jackson's. Often she will relate what is at the outset an apparently ordinary tale, including quite ordinary people, and at story's end introduce some twist that leaves the reader in a state of "wow!" Jackson was never in the best physical or mental health, and died early. She often wrote about the dark side of human mentality, as in "The Lottery." Another common theme was the striving to find a personal identity, as in the story "Maybe It Was the Car," which is found in the collection *Just an Ordinary Day*. In it, a woman— writer, wife, and mother—one day walks out on frying the supper hamburgers in a moment of self-assertion. This story is actually light and funny compared to many of her darker pieces. Another common Jackson theme—and she usually wrote about women— is individuals' perceptions of their own reality or of the world around them, and how they put their world into some workable order. Her prose style is enjoyably clean.

Jackson, Shirley. *Just an Ordinary Day*. 400p. Bantam, paper (0-553-37833-3).

Henry James
American-born, naturalized British. 1843–1916.

He had no choice in being born an American, of course, but James did choose where to spend his adult life: in Europe, primarily England. Consequently, the differences in American and European cultures were always on his mind; and the clash between New World manners and morals and those of the Old occupied much of his writing—as did the artist's difficult place in the insensitive world outside of art. James is a literary giant—no, a god, of whom readers are often afraid because of his reputation for density of prose style and ambiguity of point. Granted, his last novels are close to impenetrable; but he is incontestably an artist of the highest order, and the experience of reading his work should not be missed by any discriminating lover of literature. Approach James through his short stories and long short stories (novellas, really), in which he showed all of his talents more directly than in his novels. "The Real Thing" (in *Daisy Miller and Other Stories*) offers sensitivity, lack of obscurity, and even charm, displaying James's outstanding gifts for giving perfect shape to a story and understanding human nature. Move on to a longer piece such as "The Aspern Papers," wherein lies James's undeniably compelling power. High art, yes; but behind the rather grand facades of James's stories stand perfectly proportioned psychological portraits.

James, Henry. *The Aspern Papers and The Turn of the Screw.* 270p. Penguin, paper (0-14-043224-8).

James, Henry. *Daisy Miller and Other Stories.* 192p. Penguin, paper (0-14-006721-3).

Sarah Orne Jewett
American. 1849–1909.

The talents of Sarah Orne Jewett will amend the view of anyone who thinks any fiction writer of the nineteenth century is bound to be dry or flowery or artificial or steeped in convoluted sentence building. There is a clarity and directness to her writing that guides the reader easily through her stories. Jewett, from New England stock, wrote about the harsh beauty of the Maine landscape and the resourcefulness of the people who lived there—regular people, fishing and farming folk. A local colorist, a regionalist, Jewett nevertheless drew characters that have appeal outside the confines of their geographical perimeters. *The Country of the Pointed Firs* is her most famous work. Sometimes thought of as an episodic novel, it is actually a cycle of stories about a woman who goes to spend the summer in the little Maine coastal town of

Dunnett Landing. Through vignettes and sketches the reader comes to know the people and the sounds and smells of the place. Jewett has a wonderfully accurate ear for dialogue, for the New England dialect. She portrays these basic, hardworking people with a pinch of satire but also with a great deal of compassion and understanding. Jewett wrote many other stories besides the *Pointed Firs* sequence. One of the best is "The Only Rose," in which Mrs. Bickford tries to decide on which of the graves of her three husbands she will place her single rose.

Jewett, Sarah Orne. *The Country of the Pointed Firs and Other Stories*. 336p. Norton, paper (0-393-31137-6).

James Joyce
Irish. 1882–1941.

Joyce is certainly one of the greatest literary figures of all time. While his novels may intimidate many readers, his stories should not. *Dubliners* is the one volume of stories he wrote. These stories render key moments in ordinary, uninspired middle-class lives in the Irish capital, but in far less arcane prose than that of his novels. These carefully worded stories are far from shallow, prowling deep into seemingly still psychological waters. *Dubliners* is a cycle, a unit; taken together, in the order Joyce arranged them, the stories present a pattern of major phases through which the human life passes, from childhood onward. Little happens in Joyce's stories in terms of plot; they're more about states of mind than fast action. These Dubliners' lives are generally cheerless. But one turns to Joyce for profundity of communication. The best story in the collection, "The Dead," is universally considered by critics to be one of the most beautifully executed stories in the English language. It requires more than one reading to gather its full measure of wisdom about the human condition. It's about the annual party given by the Misses Morkan and how after one particular party their nephew had something dawn on him about his life.

Joyce, James. *Dubliners*. 182p. Bantam, paper (0-55-321380-6).

Franz Kafka
Czech. 1883–1924.

Said by at least one important critic to have been among the top two or three prose writers of the twentieth century, Kafka nonetheless is a disquieting read. In his famous novels, and likewise in his even more successful stories, his peculiar visions of inner life strike the reader as paradigmatic of the enigmas of twentieth-century life at large. Born in Prague, once a city within the borders of the Austro-Hungarian empire, Kafka died early, with his fame coming posthumously. He was abidingly concerned with the separateness of the individual—the emotional distance between a person and his or her familial, social, and political communities. His stories (which he wrote in German) have a dreamlike, almost nightmarish, quality although the ease of his style makes them easy to read. Kafka's work often reflects the universal unsettledness and fears of isolation. "In the Penal Colony," a story about an apparatus for executions, is unforgettable.

Kafka, Franz. *The Complete Stories*. 512p. Schocken, paper
  (0-8052-1055-5).

Rudyard Kipling
English. 1865–1936.

While it may come as a surprise to those who think of him only as a writer for children, generally speaking Kipling is ranked very high as a short-story writer by many critics. Some insist he's the best Britain has produced. Despite his occasional and uncomfortable lapses into what certainly seems like racist talk, Kipling's stories are every bit as exciting and intellectually stimulating as they were decades ago. He wrote of India and England and other global locales as well as all kinds of people and their predicaments. He handled dialogue brilliantly, particularly dialect, which often leaves his stories difficult to follow; in fact, his later stories are abstruse. But careful reading will reveal perfect—and perfectly sophisticated—gems of compact character and well-delineated atmosphere. Kipling's stories simultaneously entertain and challenge. "Mrs. Bathurst" is his most celebrated; it is allusive and indirect, and demands rereading. As a group of friends reminisce in South Africa, Mrs. Bathurst, a widow who keeps a bar in Auckland, New Zealand, is remembered. Kipling won the Nobel Prize in 1907.

Kipling, Rudyard. *Collected Stories.* 911p. Knopf (0-679-43592-1).

Ring Lardner
American. 1885–1933.

Lardner came to story writing from sportswriting. A great humorist and master of the vernacular, Lardner proficiently reconstructed on the printed page the way plain folks really talked, thus exerting a great influence on fiction writers coming after him. Beneath the jocularity—behind this use of everyday, up-and-down-Main-Street diction—Lardner lays common people open with razor-sharp satire. The overall effect, despite the humor flying off in all directions, is surgically precise. "The Golden Honeymoon," about an old married couple from up North gone to Florida for their golden anniversary, is both hilarious and insightful. Lardner is an easy writer for any reader to enjoy.

Lardner, Ring. *Selected Stories.* 400p. Penguin, paper (0-14-118018-8).

Mary Lavin
Irish. 1912–1995.

Although born in Massachusetts, Lavin lived in Ireland from her childhood; she was ultimately considered an Irish, not American, author. But she was acclaimed on both sides of the Atlantic as one of the premier short-story writers of the century. Her stories appeared regularly in the *New Yorker.* Her first collection of stories, *Tales from the Bective Bridge,* won the James Tait Black Memorial Prize in 1944 and established her career. Love and loneliness within family contexts are common Lavin themes, developed within realistic, often grim depictions of people not getting along or not doing what they really want to be doing. Her stories are character studies, first and foremost. Lavin, drawing on her sense of real experience, dexterously opens a small fissure in a person's makeup and lets the whole character be seen beneath. Though she had a careful, polished, at times poetically intense style, Lavin consciously wrote as if her stories weren't to be taken as formal pieces but were meant to be read aloud in a casual setting. "A Gentle Soul" is a gem; it is a truly poignant but not the least bit maudlin tale about two sisters living in rural Ireland, one of whom is secretly in love with the farmhand while the other resents any flame of passion she might see arising between her sister and the man.

Lavin, Mary. *In a Cafe: Selected Stories.* 336p. Penguin, paper (0-14-11804-04).

D. H. Lawrence
English. 1885–1930.

While Lawrence was one of the greatest novelists in the English language, his greatness also extends to the short story. Repressed sexuality and unspoken passion are subjects Lawrence wrote about voluptuously in his many stories, but in a more direct, concentrated—and thus in many readers' eyes, more effective—form than in his novels. Lawrence was the antithesis of Henry James in that he was uninterested in any sort of "artistic" considerations when it came to giving his stories shape and contour. Lawrence wanted the reader to stand up close and feel the texture of the paint he used, whereas James wanted you to stand back and admire the composition and the way the picture was matted and framed. "The Odour of Chrysanthemums" is so very Lawrentian. The wife of a coal miner is brought her husband's dead body, and only then, after he's been washed and laid out, does she really *see* him. A lovely story. Lawrence is an excellent place for readers new to short stories to begin their appreciation of the form; his stories can not fail to entice by their sensuality of emotion and language.

Lawrence, D. H. *Complete Short Stories of D. H. Lawrence.* 3v., 853p. Penguin, paper. v.1 (0-14-004382-9); v.2 (0-14-004255-5); v.3 (0-14-004383-7).

MASTERS OF THE PAST

Clarice Lispector
Brazilian. 1925–1977.

Lispector is regarded as one of the premier twentieth-century Brazilian fiction writers. Her stories offer glimpses into moments of psychological dawning—when a certain juxtaposition of events allows an individual a clearer view of the way things really are. These epiphanous moments are rendered in a variety of contexts. In one story, "Miss Algrave," a prude turns slut; in another, "The Body," a ménage à trois dissolves when a fourth partner enters the relationship; in yet another story, "He Soaked Me Up," a woman and her male hairdresser vie for the same man. The intriguing quality of a Lispector story, aside from its stylistic brilliance, is the magical weave of humor and pathos.

Lispector, Clarice. *Soulstorm.* 160p. New Directions (0-8112-1090-1); paper (0-8112-1091-X).

Jack London
American. 1876–1916.

London led a short, unrestrained life. To think of London as a writer is to think of his ever-popular 1903 novel *The Call of the Wild.* He wrote short stories in a similar vein: sinewy adventure stories, often set in the Yukon, which center on heroic individuals at odds with the forces of nature. But underneath the heavy musculature in a London story is a rough elegance, a hard sensuality—not unlike a brawny football player performing a ballet, doing well at it and enjoying it. London's ability to maintain a keen tension from first page to last, in every story, will draw readers in fully. "To Build a Fire" is quintessential London: a man out in the hostile elements, dog at his side, death looking him square in the face.

London, Jack. *To Build a Fire and Other Stories.* 400p. Bantam, paper (0-553-21335-0).

Bernard Malamud
American. 1914–1986.

With lapses into sheer fantasy, which leave his stories with an enticing, rewarding fablelike tenor, Malamud was most successful writing about New York Jews, with characters ranging from a student to an art historian to a frozen-foods salesman. Human suffering, religious intolerance, and the power of love are a few of the themes found in Malamud's deceptively simple stories. In "The Jewbird," one of his most famous, a blackbird flies one hot August evening into the open kitchen window of the New York apartment of Harry Cohen and his wife and son. The bird talks—not just mimicking human voice, but actually showing capability of reasoning and carrying on conversation—then sticks around and tries to become part of the family. The story is disarmingly charming and devastatingly wry; beneath the bizarre but uncomplicated veneer is an allegorical level: Harry's rough treatment of the bird is a paradigm for anti-Semitism as practiced by Gentiles and other Jews. Malamud was awarded the National Book Award in 1959 for his story collection *The Magic Barrel* and again in 1967 for his novel *The Fixer,* which also won him the Pulitzer Prize in the same year. As time passes, particularly with the publication of his career-encompassing *Complete Stories,* Malamud is being viewed as one of the major American story writers of the century.

Malamud, Bernard. *The Complete Stories.* 634p. Farrar
    (0-374-12639-9); Farrar/Noonday, paper (0-374-52575-7).

Katherine Mansfield
New Zealander. 1888–1923.

Born and raised in a far corner of the British Empire, Mansfield spent her adult life in England and on the Continent. In her stories, she drew upon her experiences in all these places, particularly her native New Zealand. She often wrote about lonely, emotionally isolated women and about wide-eyed children gathering impressions of adults. She wrote in a distinctive narrative voice: resonantly understated, showing a remarkable adeptness at moving smoothly in and out of a character's consciousness (which seemed quite experimental at the time she was writing, but is a standard fictional technique these days). Some contemporary critics feel Mansfield's work is too precious and ephemeral, but sensitive readers will see that the focus she places on the tender moments in peoples' lives illuminates the vulnerabilities of us all. The list of her classic stories is long indeed. It would include the paired long stories "Prelude" and "At the Bay," fiction drawn directly from Mansfield's family life back in New Zealand, as was the perfect gem "The Garden Party," in which a privileged child meets for the first time the horror of death. And "The Daughers of the Late Colonel" should not be missed. It's about the behavior and psychology of two spinster sisters in the days following the death of their domineering father.

Mansfield, Katherine. *Stories by Katherine Mansfield.* 384p.
    Random/Vintage, paper (0-679-73374-4).

W. Somerset Maugham
English. 1874–1965.

Maugham was very popular in his day and is certainly still enjoyably read today. He traveled to the far corners of the earth, and his stories reflect the experiences he garnered on these trips. Maugham's stories feature definite beginnings, middles, and endings, and their very traditional structure is upholstered in rich—often exotic—detail, all wrapped up in an engaging, urbane tone. Maugham wrote, fundamentally, about how people do or do not get along, what's underneath their attraction or disdain for each other. That doesn't mean he's a profound analyzer of personality; he is simply a careful observer of behavior. His stories are always good dramas, though, with very distinctive characters. The famous "Rain," about the South-Seas floozy Sadie Thompson, is one of his most compelling stories.

Maugham, W. Somerset. *Collected Short Stories.* 4v. Penguin,
    paper. v.1: 441p. (0-14-018589-5); v.2: 424p. (0-14-018590-9);
    v.3: 256p. (0-14-018591-7); v.4: 464p. (0-14-018592-5).

Guy de Maupassant
French. 1850–1893.

Prolific and straightforward, Maupassant wrote volumes of realistic stories about lives not always on the up-and-up—the peasant folk of his native Normandy, soldiers, small-potatoes functionaries. Chekhov was professor emeritus of the school of story writers who sample the core of a character and a situation, with little in the way of preface or introduction, and no tidy ending. Maupassant, on the other hand, preferred to compose stories that guide the reader from the shallow to the deep end and then back onto dry land. That is not to suggest Maupassant's stories are slow and tedious; on the contrary, there is not a wasted word, and a lot of action is pressed into small space. He lays open the bare essence of a character with a steady hand—what each one is really like stripped of disguise, as it were—with nothing left ambiguous. It's always obvious in a Maupassant story what's going on and how and why it ended the way it did. "The Necklace" is his most famous tale; it is set in Paris and concerns a woman from the lower middle class who, discontented with her station in life, takes a ridiculous step toward social pretension.

Maupassant, Guy de. *Selected Short Stories*. 368p. Penguin, paper (0-14-044243-X).

Carson McCullers
American. 1917–1967.

McCullers died early, at age fifty, leaving behind a not particularly extensive body of literature—but a fine one. McCullers was southern, and like her contemporary, Flannery O'Connor, another notable southern practitioner of the short story, McCullers wrote about grotesques, people afflicted physically and emotionally. Her themes include loneliness and the mental anguish that stems from love gone awry. Her unadorned style is quietly rigorous, her stories both charming and disquieting—an absorbing challenge. But further comparisons with Flannery O'Connor and other significant southern short-story writers (after O'Connor, McCullers is most often compared to Katherine Anne Porter and Eudora Welty) reveal psychological portraiture less fully realized and ironic observations less well phrased. Nevertheless, the long short story, "Ballad of the Sad Cafe" is an established and undeniably successful work. Cousin Lyman, a hunchback dwarf, walks into Miss Amelia Evans's eating and drinking establishment one day. The love relationship that ensues changes the cafe into a new place—but not forever. This peculiar, haunting story views grotesqueness of the body and the mind from a not unsympathetic stance.

McCullers, Carson. *Collected Stories of Carson McCullers*. 392p. Houghton/Mariner, paper (0-395-92505-3).

Maria Cristina Mena
Mexican-born, naturalized American. 1893–1965.

What a pleasure to discover the stories of this gifted writer who emigrated from her native Mexico as a teenager, to spend the rest of her life in New York City. Six years after her arrival, Mena began publishing short stories, the first Mexican-American woman to appear in the pages of major U.S. magazines such as *Century* and *Cosmopolitan*. She had led a privileged life in Mexico, and as a writer in the United States she wrote in English. Her story "John of God, the Water-Carrier" was anthologized in the *Best American Short Stories of 1928*. She married playwright Henry Chambers and became a good friend of D. H. Lawrence. She wrote about life in Mexico prior to and during the Revolution of 1910, as Mexico stood poised between old agrarian ways and new twentieth-century industrial ones, concerning herself particularly with such themes as the changing role of women, the economic and social influences of the United States, class hierarchy, and the revolution itself, which was to change the face and soul of Mexico forever. She wrote for American audiences, bringing them a taste of Mexican culture, usually for the first time. Her stories, in their immaculately clean style and eye for telling detail, will remind readers of the Mexican stories of another great writer, Katherine Anne Porter. One of Mena's most effective stories is "The Gold Vanity Set." Petra grew up a beautiful young woman and married well; her father-in-law runs an inn, in which Petra works. But her husband too often gets drunk, loses his temper, and beats her. "She burned many candles to the Virgin of Guadalupe that she might be granted the 'beneficio' of a more frequently sober husband." One day into her father-in-law's inn comes a group of American tourists. The tour leader leaves behind a gold vanity set, which Petra appropriates, and she believes that it is because of this instrument—a miracle of Heaven —that her husband swears never again to lay a hand on her.

Mena, Maria Cristina. *The Collected Stories of Maria Cristina Mena.* 157p. Arte Publico (1-55885-211-5).

Yukio Mishima
Japanese. 1925–1970.

Mishima's personal and political exhibitionism nearly overshadows his fiction; yet certainly his fiction is explained by his exhibitionist tendencies. He was the head of a small private military unit dedicated to pre-World War II notions of militarism and emperor worship. In 1970, upon attacking a military headquarters in Tokyo, he committed ritual suicide to the shock of the nation and the world. His story "Patriotism" gives voice to all that Mishima was "about." It is based on an actual event: a mutiny within the Japanese army in 1936, which was quashed in a few days by loyal troops. In Mishima's story, a young lieutenant has been married only six months; he and his younger wife are very much in love, enjoy each other sexually, and she understands that as the perfect military spouse she must follow her husband in death if he should lose his life. When this mutiny breaks out, the lieutenant feels his loyalties divided: between his unit, which has sided with the mutineers, and the imperial government. He commits ritual suicide and his wife, fulfilling her duty, also kills herself. The language in this piece is at once graphic and beautiful, whether in describing the couple's lovemaking or the lieutenant's self-disemboweling. The themes of emperor worship, militarism, and sensational violence that run like thick cords through this story are the themes Mishima lived and died for.

Mishima, Yukio. *Death in Midsummer and Other Stories.* 181p. New Directions; dist. by Norton, paper (0-8112-0117-1).

George Moore
Irish. 1852–1933.

It is a shame Moore is little read these days. He is of major significance in Irish literature, one of the supreme masters of the short story in the English language. Intending to be a painter, Moore eventually became involved in the turn-of-the-century renaissance of Irish culture. Out of his concern over fostering a native Irish literature came the cycle of stories *The Untilled Field,* a series of satiric depictions of the state of Irish life as he saw it, of typical people of the village and the countryside. The later *Story-Teller's Holiday* is a remarkable book, a tour de force, presenting a series of stories woven together into one long, virtually seamless narrative. It's a book you read from cover to cover, not dipping in here and there. Moore's stories are psychologically deep and culturally exact, and demonstrate why he is considered one of the finest stylists ever.

Moore, George. *Story-Teller's Holiday.* 2v. 517p. Reprint Services (0-7812-7602-0).

Moore, George. *The Untilled Field.* 346p. Ayer (0-7812-7602-0).

Wright Morris
American. 1910–1998.

Nebraskan Morris's stories are essentially of two kinds: those depicting his native Plains life, featuring distinctly etched characters that both support and dispute the stereotypical personality types of that milieu, his tone simultaneously elegiac and sardonic; and those capturing Americans staying or touring in Europe who suffer from fish-out-of-water syndrome, a situation he treats at once comically and sympathetically. Thematically, Morris is concerned with the impact of the past on the present: not simply the past events in an individual's own life, but, more markedly, the country's experiences of yesterday that lend impact to the conduct of life in general. We are creatures of our national as well as our personal pasts, Morris seems to be saying. "The Origin of Sadness," about an odd boy who grows up into an odd man, is representative of his Plains-life stories; "In Another Country" shows the reader how Morris dealt with Americans in Europe. (His novel *Field of Vision* won the 1957 National Book Award and his novel *Plains Song* won the same award in 1981.)

Morris, Wright. *Collected Stories, 1948–1986.* 274p. Godine, paper (0-87923-752-X).

Vladimir Nabokov
Russian-born, naturalized American. 1899–1977.

This giant of twentieth-century literature made his name with his novels, but the recent appearance of his collected stories reminded us all of his accomplishments in the short form. Nabokov was born into a wealthy aristocratic family in St. Petersburg. In 1919 his family fled Russia in the face of the Bolshevik Revolution; from then until 1940, when he immigrated to the United States, he lived in various European cities. Prior to his arrival on American shores, Nabokov wrote in Russian; subsesquently, he wrote in English. In 1955 he published his most famous novel, the controversial *Lolita* (which was not published in the United States until 1958). His stories, not surprisingly, are set in the places where he lived; they often deal with the themes of reconciling one's past and present. Nabokov had an unerring instinct for structure, and, of course, no one reads him without reacting to his style: luxuriant, lapidary, dazzling, almost grandiloquent. The story "La Veneziana" shows what Nabokov is about in terms of setting, tone, and style. It is a very urbane, sophisticated piece; it concerns the ways the upper crust lives, particularly their participation in the world of art connoisseurship. In an English castle in the modern day, the "Colonel" is the proprietor and an art collector; he's having as guests at the castle his art procurer and the procurer's wife, and his own son and his son's friend. (The Colonel's most recent acquisition is the painting "La Veneziana.") During the course of his visit to the castle, the Colonel's son's friend, Simon, plunges (perhaps literally?) into the magical (or is it ridiculous?) world of art collecting, observing, at the same time, sexual high-jinks. As a result, the authenticity of the Colonel's new painting is disproved. An intense, dense story you will want to—*need* to—read again.

Nabokov, Vladimir. *The Stories of Vladimir Nabokov.* 663p.
   Random/ Vintage, paper (0-679-72997-6).

Jan Neruda
Czech. 1834–1891.

Visitors to the delightful Czech capital will agree that one of the loveliest of that lovely city's streets is Neruda Street, named after one of the major figures in nineteenth-century Czech literature. Neruda was, by profession, a journalist, but he also practiced poetry, fiction writing, and the essay. He was the son of a retired soldier and grocer; his schooling gave him nationalistic tendencies, expanding his view of society and politics to radical, pan-European dimensions. He also was an important figure in the Czech society of his time; he had many love affairs, for which he was, however, criticized by the public. The book *Prague Tales* represents the epitome of Neruda as a writer: all his experiences and writerly talent coalescing into these poignant observations of the city he loved. Specifically, *Prague Tales* reports on life among the denizens of the bourgeois neighborhood of Mala Strana (the "Lesser Quarter") of nineteenth-century Prague. Neruda sprang from that neighborhood, and he immortalized it in stories that may have the sting of satire but certainly bear the mark of his greater understanding of his neighbors. Characteristic of the collection is "Evening Chitchat," in which a small group of intellectuals pass the evening in their studio meeting place, each recalling his earliest memory. It's a warm, funny story, but one with an edge, too.

Neruda, Jan. *Prague Tales.* 346p. Central European University
   Press; dist. by Oxford, paper (1-85866-058-0).

Flannery O'Connor
American. 1925–1964.

Out of the soil and citizenry of her native Georgia, O'Connor drew material for her stories. She is famous for the violence she depicts, for her dark humor, and for her abiding religious concern (i.e., the hows and whys of existence outside of divine grace and the human battle to regain it). Everywhere O'Connor looked she saw individuals who were morally impaired and physically imperfect. These were not lives high in substance and purpose, yet she wrote about them in a tragicomic vein. The reader laughs, yet with understanding. O'Connor possessed a marvelous ear for dialogue; her style was straightforward, rock solid. Her *Complete Stories* won the 1972 National Book Award. The story "A Good Man Is Hard to Find" is vintage O'Connor, about a family on an automobile trip to Florida. Along a rough country road, the car takes a flip, and the family is . . . yes, it's true, wiped out by a gang of desperadoes who happen along.

O'Connor, Flannery. *The Complete Stories*. 555p. Farrar
(0-374-12752-2); paper (0-374-51536-0).

Frank O'Connor
Irish. 1903–1966.

Sean O'Faolain
Irish. 1900–1991.

Liam O'Flaherty
Irish. 1896–1984.

Of the same generation, this triumvirate accomplished lasting results as they carried the torch of Irish short-story writing handed them from George Moore and James Joyce and passed it on to contemporary Irish story writers.

With marvelous humor and poignancy, O'Connor wrote stories in a personal tone, as if he were actually sitting down and spinning a yarn aloud. There is an immediacy in his writing, a sense of the shared anecdote passed down to the next generation. He evokes with inherent articulateness the atmosphere of provincial Ireland, rendering indelibly the nature of the populace, from children to old folks. O'Connor created wonderful, idiosyncratic characters who handle the problems in their rough lives very much in their own fashion. Read "Guests of the Nation" to see how Irish politics imbued his writing, "The Drunkard" for its humor, and "The Long Road to Ummera" to be moved to tears.

O'Faolain's stories are a lot less like yarns than O'Connor's. O'Faolain stands back a bit, in order to gain a clearer analytical perspective of the socioeconomic/political environment of Ireland. His characters are more finely chiseled, the atmosphere and psychology slightly keener, his style more lovely in its imagery. O'Faolain is, then, the finer artist of the two—but perhaps less charming than O'Connor. "Lovers of the Lake" is among his most popular and most rewarding stories. It's about a man and woman—lovers—who go on a pilgrimage.

Of the three, O'Flaherty is generally the briefer, denser, more poetic writer. Without much development of scene and character, he goes in for the hard punch, delivered in sharp language. O'Flaherty offers quick dramas set in ordinary domestic surroundings, in drab ordinary communities, within lives led with no luxury and at the mercy of the elements. He's more instinctual than O'Faolain and O'Connor—writing more from the guts than with heart or mind. Uniquely, and without schmaltz or contrivance, O'Flaherty crafted some tales featuring animals as main characters. "The Wounded Cormorant" is among the best of these.

O'Connor, Frank. *Collected Stories*. 736p. Random/Vintage, paper (0-394-71048-7).

O'Faolain, Sean. *Short Stories of Sean O'Faolain*. 1,304p. Dufour Editions (0-90167-230-3).

O'Flaherty, Liam. *The Collected Stories*. 3v. St. Martin's, paper. v.1: 366p. (0-312-22903-8); v.2: 396p. (0-312-22904-6); v.3: 397p. (0-312-22905-4).

John O'Hara
American. 1905–1970.

Some critics deem O'Hara one of the best short-story writers the United States has produced; others see his fiction as just good journalism. Either way, he has proven abidingly popular. O'Hara wrote many stories over a long career. Dialogue is the most important aspect of an O'Hara story—he always got the vocabulary, phonetics, cadences, and syntax just right, no matter what the socioeconomic group, from the moneyed class to the upper middle class, to ordinary working people and even show-business types. This skill enabled him to conjure up a vivid character in brief space. O'Hara supplemented his ear for dialogue with a keen consciousness of social trappings, for instance, the cars, the neighborhoods, the kinds of dwelling. He was very much in touch with the many walks of American life. Whether a story such as "The Doctor's Son" is art or simply accurate reportage, it can't be denied that O'Hara is eminently easy to read, to understand, to be entertained by. O'Hara's novel *Ten North Frederick* won the 1956 National Book Award.

O'Hara, John. *Collected Stories of John O'Hara.* 414p. Random (0-394-54083-2); paper (0-394-74311-3).

Dorothy Parker
American. 1893–1967.

Parker is remembered as one of the greatest "quipsters" in American literary history. She was a founding member of the Algonquin Round Table, that circle of literati and wits that gathered daily at the Algonquin Hotel in Manhattan for lunch and exchange of banter and quotable quotes. She wrote short stories, poetry, and reviews (of dramas and books, for *Vanity Fair,* the *New Yorker,* and *Esquire*); and also plays. Parker's distinctive voice in her writings helped set the tone of the *New Yorker,* which began publication in 1925. But she was a troubled soul; her biting humor barely masked great personal unhappiness. In later years she battled alcoholism and writer's block. Her short stories are not so ephemeral as her reputation often now estimates them; they remain sharp, witty, keen satires of changing social and sexual mores, every one of them still readable today. They were well constructed; Parker had great instinct for the short-story form, its restrictions suiting her material and her voice. She practiced greatly economic writing, very trenchant; her descriptions of people and environments very neatly and quickly hit the nail on the head. She often focused on upper-class Manhattan women and the distresses of their lives: they didn't work, and booze and entertaining were not fulfilling. Some of her stories are dramatic monologues, at which she was especially adept. Of course, given her own often downcast temperament, a sadness permeates her stories. The story "Big Blonde" is one of her most famous ones and certainly one of her most polished portraits: in this instance, of Mrs. Hazel Morse, a fur-loving peroxide blonde. Hazel is a character type that Parker loved to satirize, but the picture is exquisitely wrought.

Parker, Dorothy. *Complete Stories.* 447p. Penguin, paper (0-14-018939-4).

Cesare Pavese
Italian. 1908–1950.

Pavese was considered one of the major European writers of his day, but he is little read now, which is unfortunate, for he remains a fascinating short-story writer. Pavese served as an editor at the Turin publishing house he cofounded; he was imprisoned in the 1930s for anti-Fascist activities. His personality could not be described as anything but dark. Beset by abiding unhappiness, very sensitive by nature, not good at relating to others, and not particularly well disposed toward women, Pavese committed suicide at age forty-one. But his stark writing reflects his attendant enjoyment of poetry writing. In his stories he writes of the emotional abysses into which the human psyche can plunge; he understands the mental free fall into anguish, and he finds compassion for those in a downward spiral. "Misogyny" is a characteristic Pavese story, taking place in a remote little tavern "under the shadow of the mountains." A young man and woman enter; their car has run out of gas. It soon becomes obvious they are fleeing, from what exactly we never are privy to. The tavern keeper aids in their flight across the border into France, without ever learning what prompted it. Dark, brooding, mysterious—typical Pavese fare.

Pavese, Cesare. *Stories*. 412p. Ecco, paper (0-88001-124-6).

Edgar Allan Poe
American. 1809–1849.

Poe makes a good vocabulary lesson—the reader is bound to head for the dictionary at some point while reading him. But that's not to imply that reading Poe is to engage in work, nor to imply that since he's good for you he must be dry as dust. On the contrary, Poe's stories of detection, of horror, of adventure, of science fiction, while historically important in the evolution of the short story, remain vital reading today. The darkness of Poe's soul pervades all of his stories, leaving them disturbing yet undeniably absorbing. Atmosphere was his strong suit; the threatening feeling he stirred into so many of his stories fairly wafts off every page and into the reader's senses. "The Tell-Tale Heart" is arguably the best short story of its kind in the English language. This is a riveting story of madness and murder: a man driven crazy by hearing the still-beating heart of the man he murdered and whose body he hid beneath the floorboards of his victim's room.

Poe, Edgar Allan. *Selected Tales*. 352p. Oxford, paper (0-19-283224-7).

Katherine Anne Porter
American. 1890–1980.

Porter lived a long while but published relatively little. Nevertheless, what she may have lacked in quantity she more than compensated for in quality. Porter is often referred to as a writer's writer because of the shimmering beauty of her seemingly effortless style and her graceful use of symbol. Consequently, she deserves a much wider readership than many other writers. Her crystal-clear style is universally inviting; and, as far as her symbolism goes, it works so smoothly on a subconscious level that readers can benefit from the effect without ever having to pick a symbol up off the page and say, "I found one." Porter was from the South and traveled in—and adored—Mexico. She effectively transferred to the written page her deeply held reactions to these places. The sequence of very short stories called "The Old Order" leaves an indelible impression of her deep emotional commitment to her family's past within the context of the passing of the gentility of the late-nineteenth-century Old South. Her stories set in Mexico—outstandingly "María Concepción" and "Flowering Judas"—evoke place and character with startling precision. *Porter's Collected Stories* won the 1966 Pulitzer Prize as well as the National Book Award for the same year.

Porter, Katherine Anne. *The Collected Stories of Katherine Anne Porter.* 495p. HBJ, paper (0-15-618876-7).

V. S. Pritchett
English. 1900–1997.

Many critics and well-read general readers claim Pritchett to have been one of the best English short-story writers of recent decades. He was astonishingly prolific, a true man of letters: at home in most literary forms. But his fame—both critical and popular— will always rest on his numerous short stories. In *Midnight Oil,* the second volume of his classic autobiography, Pritchett states that the short story's concise form "concentrates an impulse that is essentially poetic." Every story he wrote showed the beauty of this poetic impulse. With rich subtlety, he observed moments in ordinary experience—in lives of typical working and middle-class people—and found the idiosyncrasies that, on one hand, make characters unique, but, on the other hand, indicate a universality in human frailties. Pritchett had a marvelous sense of comedy, leavened with compassion. "The Saint," both exemplary and outstanding, probes a teenage boy's loss of faith. And the ever-popular "The Camberwell Beauty" is a keen, deeply resonant exploration of the eccentric characters involved in the London antique business. "Many Are Disappointed" shows Pritchett as the fine craftsman that he was; this story follows four male cyclists as they stop off en route for a beer, only to find the establishment serves only tea. "Many are disappointed," the tavern keeper admits.

Pritchett, V. S. *Collected Stories*. 310p. Random, paper (0-394-52417-7).

Jean Rhys
West Indian. 1894–1979.

Born and raised on the Caribbean island of Dominica, Rhys spent her adult life mostly in England and France; and it is those three locales in which her stories are generally set. Rhys dropped out of the literary scene after a very successful publishing run in the 1930s; but before her death her greatness had been restored. In her novels and short stories, she surveyed the internal states of loneliness and victimization with economical fluency and ironic beauty. The most beguiling aspect of her stories is that, while a tone of ennui rises from them (as if Rhys couldn't help interjecting a blasé attitude about writing them), each word, each phrase, each sentence, on second glance, has obviously been chosen with care to deliver the exact mood of distractedness and dejection. "Mannequin," a story of luscious brevity, concerns a young woman newly hired as a model at the salon of a Paris couturiere.

Rhys, Jean. *The Collected Short Stories*. 403p. Norton, paper, (0-393-30625-9).

Kate Roberts
Welsh. 1891–1985.

A member of the Welsh Nationalist Party, Roberts eschewed English to write her trenchant stories in her native tongue. She explored—explained, perhaps, is the best word—the world in which she grew up: the poor quarrying villages in the mountains of Wales. Not surprisingly, then, it is common people struggling against poverty who populate her stories. "The Red-Letter Day" unbluntedly reveals Roberts's masterful traits. One day, the first day of summer, a ten-shilling note arrives at the house of Rachel Annie and her father, a gift from Rachel's uncle. In their dire straits, such benevolence should be cause for relief; but there were so many things about the house needing repair, "since one couldn't do it all with ten shillings, it was better not to do anything." So Rachel and her father decide to use the money for a day off. Rachel takes the train into Cardiff, the capital, and has a *capital* time, forgetting herself and her problems in all the excitement of the place. Inevitably, of course, the trip home returns her to the harshness of her real existence. Exemplary of Roberts, this story is composed in a deliberate, clean style; it is heartfelt without being mawkish; and it is Katherine Mansfield-esque in its ability to let a small incident so resonantly speak of the condition of a person's entire life.

Roberts, Kate. *The World of Kate Roberts: Selected Stories 1925 1981.* 372p. Temple University (0 87722 794 2); paper (0-87722-795-0).

Saki
Scottish. 1870–1916.

Want a good laugh? Not just to crack a smile, but to let loose with a real out-loud laugh? Pick up the incorrigible Saki, pseudonym of Hector Hugh Munro, and turn to "The Stampeding of Lady Bastable," one of the stories in the collection *The Chronicles of Clovis.* In the space of a few pages, for about two minutes, the reader delights in Saki's mischievousness, his near-wickedness. A Saki story is short and tight, rendered in a style arch in tone and lacquered with sarcasm. Social pretension and pomposity are the targets of his jabs, and he hilariously deflated such absurd attitudes. His wit could be mean, even grim; but all his stories are pleasurable, if perversely so. Like listening to a friend who is constantly mocking people behind their backs, one reads Saki feeling guilty, conspiratorial—but not about to miss any of the devastatingly funny remarks. Saki's stories are distinguished by beautiful concision: time, place, and character are all conveyed in their essence with minimal elaboration.

Saki. *The Complete Saki.* 456p. Penguin, paper (0-14-118078-1).

Isaac Bashevis Singer
Polish-born, naturalized American. 1904–1991.

Singer, winner of the 1978 Nobel Prize, had an expansive personality, and it shows in his stories, as if each one of them were saying to readers, "Come join me in the fun of storytelling." With an appreciative sense of the wonders of human nature, Singer wrote about the power of love and sex despite the hardships life may deliver. His stories are embedded in Jewish-Polish folklore; set in the Polish historical past (nineteenth and early-twentieth-century shtetls) and in New York City; and limn the lives of religious people, simple people, old folks, writers, tradespeople. Singer wrote his stories first in Yiddish, then translated them into English; but Yiddish speech patterns and rhythms remain, leaving his fablelike voice. Singer's works often involve the supernatural or simply fantastic, though realistically conveyed, situations. Take, for example, "Yentl the Yeshiva Boy," the basis of Barbra Streisand's 1983 movie, *Yentl.* In it, a young woman in late-nineteenth-century Poland poses as a boy so she can go to Yeshiva school and study the Torah and Talmud. Its simple charm assures the reader that such a far-fetched situation is not beyond credence.

Singer, Isaac Bashevis. *The Collected Stories of Isaac Bashevis Singer.* 614p. Farrar/Noonday, paper (0-374-51788-6).

E. OE. Somerville and Martin Ross
Anglo-Irish. (Somerville) 1858–1949.
(Ross) 1862–1915.

Edith Somerville and Violet Martin (pseudonymously Martin Ross) were cousins and extremely successful collaborators in writing novels and short stories. Their fiction reflected their roots: the Protestant Ascendancy, the English-descent land-owning class in Ireland, which, at the time Somerville and Ross lived and wrote—the late nineteenth and early twentieth centuries—was on the decline. They wrote a series of comic short stories, originally published in three volumes, about the adventures of one Major Sinclair Yeates, a Resident Magistrate sent from England to the west of Ireland, officially to administer justice. As it turns out, he becomes embroiled time and time again in the chicanery of the native Irish—and emerges as if *he's* the one lacking sophistication. The entire world of Anglo-Irish Protestant overlords and submissive Catholic tenants is evoked with knee-slapping humor—but no meanness. Every story is finely composed, with quick pacing and wonderful dialogue; the blarney flying in all directions. The story "Great-Uncle McCarthy" sets the stage and introduces Yeates and other recurring characters.

Somerville, E. OE. and Martin Ross. *Some Experiences of an Irish R. M.* 232p. J. S. Sanders, paper (1-87994140-6).

Jean Stafford
American. 1915–1979.

Although her *Collected Stories* won the 1970 Pulitzer Prize, the late Jean Stafford nevertheless is little recognized outside the narrow circle of avid and serious fiction readers and writers. Without a doubt, she should be sampled by anyone interested in the compellingness of the short-story form. Stafford probed squarely into what she perceived as the arid side of life: emotional detachment from people, either self-inflicted or inflicted by others. She wrote often of lonely children easily bruised by adults, or of adults remembering such a childhood. Settings include Colorado, where Stafford grew up, and the places she knew as an adult: New York, Boston, and Europe. Stafford was a lover of big words, long sentences, lots of clauses; she was not one to present an idea head on, but, rather, to circle around it and gradually pry it open to full exposure. "Children Are Bored on Sunday" is a famous story and justifiably so. When Emma encounters social acquaintance Alfred Eisenberg on a Sunday afternoon at the Metropolitan Museum in

New York, she is sent into an introspective inquiry into her current state of solitude.

Stafford, Jean. *The Collected Stories of Jean Stafford.* 463p. University of Texas, paper (0-29271145-X).

John Steinbeck
American. 1902–1968.

Steinbeck lived in California and wrote of it sympathetically. He is certainly a titan in twentieth-century American literature (winner of the 1962 Nobel Prize); but as magnificent as his best novels are, among them, of course, *The Grapes of Wrath* (which won the 1940 Pulitzer Prize), they should not eclipse his short stories. Start with the frequently anthologized "The Chrysanthemums," about a rancher's wife whose low-burning inner flame is renewed one day by an itinerant pot-mender, only to have her heart broken; or the four-story cycle *The Red Pony,* a moving depiction of the circumstances that thrust a boy on a California ranch headlong into maturity. Steinbeck was always one to focus on the poor and the outcast, on the more elementary levels of social existence as opposed to the more urban and technological and cultural aspects. He wrote of men and women taking their lumps in the hard physical and emotional environment of the underprivileged. Steinbeck's style is diverse, but it is essentially a balanced play of directness and studiedness; a sort of raw elegance.

Steinbeck, John. *The Long Valley.* 320p. Penguin, paper (0-14-018745-6).

Robert Louis Stevenson
Scottish. 1850–1894.

Stevenson suffered from ill health and died young. He led a "bohemian" life in reaction to his strict upbringing; he is buried on Samoa in the South Pacific, where he established residency. Stevenson was a prolific writer in several forms: a man of letters. He wrote perennially popular novels such as the adventure romances *Kidnapped* and *Treasure Island,* but he was also among the first of the important British story writers. At the top of the list of Stevenson stories is the famous longer tale of dual personality, *The Strange Case of Dr. Jekyll and Mr. Hyde,* based on the double life of Edinburgh's notorious Deacon Brodie. It demonstrates perfectly Stevenson's propensity for examining moral conflicts in smooth, unobtrusive elegance. His stories roamed the globe from his native Scotland to Hawaii, through the centuries back to the Middle Ages. His characters ranged from royalty to poets to sailors. In all of his stories, Stevenson offered compelling plot; and, with his superior control in achieving a certain atmospheric effect, he could easily put his reader into just the appropriate mood.

Stevenson, Robert Louis. *The Strange Case of Dr. Jekyll and Mr. Hyde and Other Stories.* 304p. Penguin, paper (0-14-043117-9).

Rabindranath Tagore
Indian. 1861–1941.

The 1913 winner of the Novel Prize for Literature (India's only winner of that prize) was born in Bengal into a prominent political and cultural family. He wrote distinguished poetry as well as fiction. Though son of a rich man, Tagore identified closely with simple lives around him; his intense love of rural Bengal, its people (villagers and gentry alike), and its geography is beautifully obvious in his stories. His vivid pictures of Bengali life range in method from realistic to fantastic; either way, the reader gains a rich feel for Tagore's mysterious and magnificent native land. "The Postmaster" is a realistic and poignant story about a village functionary and where his heart leads him; while "The Angry Stones" takes place on a train trip during which a stranger relates to the narrator a lush tale of hauntedness.

Tagore, Rabindranath. *Selected Short Stories.* 336p. Penguin, paper (0-14-018854-1).

Peter Taylor
American. 1917–1994.

Despite his lack of an extensive popular following, Taylor commanded high critical respect for his short stories. (His novels, too, were greatly respected; *A Summons to Memphis* won the 1987 Pulitzer Prize.) He wrote of his native region, the southern United States—Tennessee, to be specific—in a cool, unflustered style that easily caught the reader's attention without confusion or hesitation. Taylor's work stands poised between gentle sarcasm and an elegiac tone in its depictions of the southern gentility of a bygone age— the "Old South"—poised against the new values of the modern industrial South. His characters are ruling class: professional people, old landed families, politicians. (His grandfather had been both a U.S. senator and governor of Tennessee.) His stories' abiding hospitality, their sensitive but unsentimental comprehension of the nature of relationships—between lovers, between parent and child, and between races—give them an enduring beauty. His collection *The Old Forest* was awarded the PEN/Faulkner Award as the best work of fiction of 1995. The story from which the collection takes its name sums up Taylor's themes and style. The narrator, now a college professor but a former cotton broker, recounts a tragic event that occurred in his younger life.

Taylor, Peter. *The Collected Stories of Peter Taylor.* 535p. Penguin, paper (0-14-008361-8).

Ivan Turgenev
Russian. 1818–1883.

Turgenev was a great influence on English and American short-story writers, a seminal figure in the development of the modern short story. His *Sportsman's Sketches* (included in the Penguin edition, *Hunter's Album)* is a series of vignettes published individually between 1847 and 1851 in the Russian journal *The Contemporary* and then in book form in 1852. With poetic intensity, Turgenev captured moments in a nobleman's perambulations through the countryside and, in the process, distilled much of the negative side of nineteenth-century Russian life—namely, the repression of the peasantry (serfdom not being abolished until 1861). With acute irony, Turgenev imbedded a subtle, sympathetic understanding of tyrannized people within lovely descriptions of nature's comforts and surprises.

Turgenev, Ivan. *Sketches from a Hunter's Album*. 416p. Penguin, paper (0-14-044522-6).

Mark Twain
American. 1835–1910.

Samuel Langhorne Clemens, Mark Twain, is a permanent fixture in the pantheon of great American fiction writers, noted primarily for his novels *The Adventures of Tom Sawyer* and *The Adventures of Huckleberry Finn*. He is esteemed as a humorist, proficient in writing in the colloquial voice of plain river and frontier folk, the practitioner of a shining, clear style. In critical and popular minds, Twain's stories form rather an adjunct to his famous novels. Nonetheless, they are so very stimulating—yarns spun humorously, satirically, and enduringly. There is a delicious personal feel to his stories, as if Twain were lounging right beside the reader, chair tipped back, feet up, poking fun at people he's encountered or heard tell of. Among his best short works are "The Man That Corrupted Hadleyburg," about a gambler who takes revenge on a smugly pious town for their insult, and "The Notorious Jumping Frog of Calaveras County," in which Twain's oral style of storytelling is best demonstrated.

Twain, Mark. *The Complete Short Stories of Mark Twain*. 679p. Bantam, paper (0-553-21195-1).

Glenway Wescott
American. 1901–1987.

Wescott was part of the expatriate group of American writers who lived and wrote in Paris between the world wars. In 1928, he published a superb cycle of stories entitled *Good-Bye Wisconsin*. Preceding the ten stories is an introduction in which Wescott shares his remembrance of a trip back home to

Wisconsin by train one Christmas Eve. He recollects how on this occasion he once again found himself pondering the restraining nature of small midwestern towns. In the stories that follow, Wescott works out variations on this theme. With a metaphoric richness of style that came to be his trademark, he demonstrates a scrupulous sensitivity to the individual's need to throw over the traces of a monotonous life in order to enjoy existence a degree or two closer to the edge. His Midwest, in these stories, emerges as a place where people too often do not take risks—but grow tremendously as individuals when and if they gather the courage and embark on some risk-taking. Of the ten stories, "The Runaways" and "The Dove Came Down" best relate these sentiments.

Wescott, Glenway. *Good-Bye Wisconsin.* 346p. Ayer (0-8369-3739-2).

Edith Wharton
American. 1862–1937.

Wharton was brought up in the narrow world of late-nineteenth-century New York society. It's no surprise, then, that she wrote of that milieu of comfort and power. She was a friend of Henry James and is often referred to as a "disciple" of his, in light of her penchant for elegant investigations of the manners of the well-to-do. But Wharton wrote with a more serrated edge than is found in James's smoother, cleaner dissections of social steps and missteps. In other words, she takes *obvious* satiric jabs at social posturing, which sometimes strike the reader as unnecessarily mean-spirited. But Wharton's language is luminously sculpted, and her sense of the short-story form's power-in-concentration is impeccable. "Roman Fever" is a chilling story—Wharton deftly manipulates the reader, then concludes with a literary slap in the face. In it, two women, American tourists, spend the afternoon on a terrace overlooking the Forum in Rome, battling about their pasts.

Wharton, Edith. *Roman Fever and Other Stories.* 236p. Scribner (0-68417011-6); paper (0-68482990-8).

4

Contemporary Masters

Good—no, masterful—story writing continues into the present day. Experimentation flourishes in Latin America. In Great Britain, where traditions die hard, stories in very traditional veins continue to be written. This is true in Ireland as well and, generally speaking, the world over.

In the United States of the 1980s, the newest trend was minimalism—the writer utilizing extremely spare prose. Plots were minimal—readers simply found themselves cast into the midst of a dramatic confrontation of some sort. No introduction; no great elaboration of scene and character; just a minimum of development. The reader learned only what was absolutely essential about people and their plights. The sentences that delivered this information were pared down, too. Subject, verb. Subject, verb. Few complete sentence constructions, few modifiers. Very little in the way of embellishment or decoration. A minimalist sentence was sort of like a room done in high tech. The starkness, the very absence of style, *was* the style.

But minimalism is no longer in vogue. In fact, the great Latin American writer Isabel Allende, in a recent interview, indicated that minimalism is dying, and, for her, it is about time. A time to return to "artistry in words."

What follows is a selective list of the short-story writers at work today whom I consider the most interesting, the ones most likely to last.

Lee Abbott
American. 1947–

Abbott, a professor of English at Ohio State University, is a prolific, award-winning short-story writer. He has never written a novel, and he need not do so for the sake of his literary reputation; his esteem as a fiction writer is well established by his superior short stories. Southwestern settings predominate in Abbott's work, which often features middle-aged men who served in Vietnam and are now confused as they try to find their way through life's travails, particularly those stemming from marital problems. His stories are grounded in regular situations (that is, in predicaments that are not uncommon in today's world) and they present outwardly regular people; but it is Abbott's habit to isolate a certain idiosyncratic character trait that stamps these individuals as unique in their own particular fashion. Abbott is distinguished by his vigorous yet poised writing; he carefully composes prose of sheer—not showy—eloquence. ("'There are women I slept with,' he said, his voice mostly air and throat"—from the story "Notes I Made on the Man I Was.") His writing is riddled with humor, which occasionally has the ring of mockery. In fact, readers may find some of his stories too clever and seeming to have a writers-workshop "slickness" about them, as if they were built from prefabricated pieces from a story-writing kit, rather than made to order by hand and brick by brick. The story "The End of Grief" is quintessential Abbott. A boy grows to manhood in the face of a father obsessed with the Bataan Death March in April of 1942, during which the father's brother lost his life; the father raises the boy as if he were nothing but the spitting image of his long-deceased uncle. But eventually the father comes to "the end of grief."

Abbott, Lee. *Strangers in Paradise.* 255 p. Random, paper
  (0-814-20712-X).

Chinua Achebe
Nigerian. 1930–

With the outward simplicity and intrinsic wisdom of a traditional fable, Achebe's story "The Madman" takes the fascinated and delighted reader into the ways of village life in his native Nigeria. The title character "was drawn to markets and straight roads," and he discovers that both urges can be satisfied by the market villages of Afo and Eke, which are linked by a highway. He can spend his days going from one village to the other via the highway. One day, though, in search of a drink of water, he leaves the highway and spots Nuike, "a man of high standing" in another village, bathing in the stream. To cover his own often-ridiculed nakedness, the madman swipes Nuike's cloth, having recognized Nuike as a man who had previously taunted him. A chase ensues: Nuike running after the madman to get his cloth back. In the process, Nuike himself loses his reason and it takes a while for his madness to be cured. But Nuike is never the same; in fact, he loses his high social standing. Frequently cited as a potential recipient of the Nobel Prize, Achebe laces his realism with humor to explain the attitudes and activities of his homeland. His lucid, penetrating voice speaks from both heart and mind.

Achebe, Chinua. *Girls at War and Other Stories*. 120p. Doubleday/ Anchor, paper (0-385-41896-5).

Isabel Allende
Chilean. 1942–

Born in Lima, Peru, the daughter of a Chilean diplomat on assignment there, Allende grew up in her native country, in time becoming a journalist. She is the niece of Salvador Allende, Marxist president of Chile who died in 1973 in a coup against his regime; after the death of her uncle, she emigrated to Venezuela, began writing fiction there, and now lives in the United States. *The Stories of Eva Luna* is a Latin American version of *One Thousand and One Nights;* prompted by her lover in post-coital bliss, Eva Luna, the main character from Allende's earlier novel, spends the rest of the night spinning yarns for his amusement. The stories she composes are tales of love—love gone wrong, and sometimes love gone right. They are at once fantastic and sensuously realistic. "The Little Heidelberg" is heartbreaking. It is a mystical piece about a tavern where old folks go to dine and dance. El Capitan is a long-term habitue, and after forty years of hesitation he is finally compelled to ask Nina Eloisa to dance. But it's too late, she's . . . No, the ending simply *can't* be given away!

Allende, Isabel. *The Stories of Eva Luna.* 288p. Bantam, paper
  (0-553-57535-X).

Margaret Atwood
Canadian. 1939–

Atwood writes about the problem of the individual connecting with others, the difficulty of maintaining connections once they are established, and the occasional necessity of backing away from connections. Her stories stun the reader with brilliance of thought and expression. Most of Atwood's stories—"The Whirlpool Rapids" and "Walking on Water," for instance—are lean and direct, full of punch. The beauty of her sentences is bolstered by an immaculate sense of form, with every word leading to a preordained effect. Other stories—for example, "Bluebeard's Egg"—are weakened by their long descriptions of the characters and their situations. Atwood spends too much time filling in the reader on peripheral matters. The joy of reading her polished, luminous prose is strained in these less tightly composed pieces.

Atwood, Margaret. *Bluebeard's Egg.* 256p. Anchor, paper
  (0-385-49104-2).

Rick Bass
American. 1958–

Bass is hot these days, and rightly so. His nature essays brim with indelible images and heartfelt passions. But more to the point here, he is also an extraordinary short-story writer, one of uncommon sensitivity to conditions of the heart and psyche as well as to the natural environment that people too often ignore. Current popularity, at least in Bass's case, certainly does not preclude a lasting reputation; you can be certain that his story collections will be in print permanently and that individual stories of his will be widely anthologized. Mark these words: Bass is here to stay. Imbedded in his stories, like DNA in a cell's nucleus, are the keys to human nature. Underscored with a charming sense of humor ("When she kissed you it was like going swimming in the ocean on a hot day with a bunch of people standing around applauding"—from "Mississippi"), his stories reflect an abiding interest in and concern for natural history and, concomitantly, environmentalism. (Bass now lives on a remote ranch in northern Montana.) Add to all this a marvelously felicitous style, and you've got stories with great literary appeal, from which readers learn about cooperation and collusion with our natural settings. One perfect example of his style and substance is "Days of Heaven," in which the particularities of plot and character are artfully rooted in the issues of nature preservation. A man commissioned as caretaker for a mansion built on a ranch deep in remote Montana defines his caretaking role by plotting to stop plans for "developing" the valley. He is intent on pursuing "my days of heaven—I'd gotten used to them, and I wanted to defend them and protect them, even if they weren't mine in the first place, even if I'd never owned them." A beautifully effective story with scenes that are hard to forget.

Bass, Rick. *In the Loyal Mountains.* 168p. Houghton Mifflin/Mariner, paper (0-395-87747-4).

Bass, Rick. *The Watch.* 190p. Norton, paper (0-393-31135-X).

Anne Beattie
American. 1947–

Beattie appears regularly in the *New Yorker.* In an assertive, intelligent voice, she probes attitudes and postures taken by persons in love— from the point at which it springs up, to its dying out. Beattie populates her stories with upper-middle-class adults who were brimming with causes in the 1960s, but now, at the turn of the millennium, are only angst-filled. Simple sentences are Beattie's trademark; as a whole, they strike resonant chords. Like brief encounters between individuals in life, her stories are not neatly wrapped up with tidy endings; they are subtle, with a leisurely air but without a hard-and-fast denouement. "Secrets and Surprises" shows Beattie's skills to good advantage. The young woman narrator, divorced, moves from

New York to Connecticut; but it's not a retreat, for life continues to display its inherent round of secrets and surprises.

Beattie, Anne. *Secrets and Surprises*. 302p. Random/Vintage, paper (0-679-73193-8).

T. Coraghessan Boyle
American. 1948–

To Boyle goes the award for most originality and ingenuity of any contemporary American short-story writer; only the versatility of Latin American story writers—Francisco Hinojosa, for example—can come close to his consistent creativity. To read the incomparable "Ike and Nina" is to immediately appreciate Boyle's talent. The narrator of this story can now, now that "the principals [have] passed into oblivion . . . reveal the facts surrounding one of the most secretive and spectacular love affairs of our time." The specific time the narrator is remembering is September 1959, when he was an assistant to one of President Eisenhower's junior staffers. Ike more or less plucks him from the White House corps to perform special duties: namely, to act as go-between between the President and his lover, Nina Khrushchev, wife of the Soviet premier. This story is a delicious example of one of Boyle's specialties, the political parody. Here is a definite clue as to the tongue-in-cheek nature of the narrator's voice, in this instance describing Nina Khrushchev: "this vision in the doorway, simple, unadorned, elegant, this true princess of the earth." Huh? Remember what Madame K. actually looked like? Anyway, Boyle's comic range is amazing; his mocking, lacerating voice knows no bounds. Contemporary society as well as the historical past is a frequent "victim" of his skewering. Beneath his barbs, though, sings a style beautiful in its descriptive vibrancy and laden with exquisite metaphors. Every story is exacting in detail, no matter when or where it is set. Boyle is to be entertained by, but he is also to be supremely admired. Oh, and don't miss "Greasy Lake." You won't recover from the images conjured up by this special story for a long time to come.

Boyle, T. Coraghessan. *T. C. Boyle Stories*. 691p. Viking (0-670-87960-6); Penguin, paper (0-14-028091-X).

Ray Bradbury
American. 1920–

Bradbury is the author of several very famous novels, among them *Fahrenheit 451* (1953), *Dandelion Wine* (1957), and *Something Wicked This Way Comes* (1962). But his most famous work is *The Martian Chronicles* (1950), which is actually a cycle of interrelated short stories. In fact, he is most effective as a writer of short stories. And, despite his reputation as a masterful science fiction writer, his short stories go beyond SF to include gothic horror, social criticism of contemporary life (and, with that, commentary on technology), crime, and reminiscences of midwestern life and childhood. Bradbury refuses to categorize himself, preferring instead to call himself a writer of ideas, a magician and illusionist. Many critics, and many book review sources, have treated him as a hack; the truth is, though, he is a far better writer than that. He is quite lyrical, in fact; he's fully adept at strong sensory images, rich metaphors, and poetic language of impressive intensity. Coming of age—the reach for maturity—is a common Bradbury theme; and this theme is treated with particular sensitivity. The fantasy "The April Witch" is prime Bradbury. It is spring, and the teenage girl Cecy wants to be in love; and Cecy is capable of inhabiting every living or nonliving thing as she floats over, around, and through this spring night. "Hers was an adaptably quick mind flowing unseen upon Illinois winds on this one evening of her life when she was just seventeen." To that end— to find love—Cecy enters the body of Ann Leary, and the consequences are very touching.

Bradbury, Ray. *Classic Stories I.* 348p. Bantam, paper (0-553-28637-4).

Michael Chabon
American. 1963–

Chabon is roundly considered one of the premier literary writers of his young generation. Equally adept at the novel and the short story, he is regarded, first and foremost, as a stylist. His beautifully wrought sentences absolutely sing with breathtaking metaphors; his descriptive passages are marvelously rich without being cloying or mannered. His ability to create an image with poetically precise, resonant, and even startling language will compel the reader through one story after another. He offers moments of sheer genius in capturing a person, scene, and situation; he offers brand new views of life and people's peculiarities, within very original plots that aren't simply retreading of tired old terrain worked over so many other times by other writers. Domestic life is his landscape—specifically, dysfunctional family and social relationships. His explorations of these environments are accomplished with wit, sensitivity, and empathy; and his dialogue is consistently right on the money in terms of realism. "S Angel" is a typical Chabon story: so amusing, so beautifully done. It is about a young man attending his cousin's wedding; there he meets an inviting but messed-up older woman and is forced to come "face to face with the distinct possibility that not only would he never find the one he was meant to find, but that no one else ever did, either."

Chabon, Michael. *A Model World and Other Stories.* 207p. Avon, paper (0-380-71099-4).

Sandra Cisneros
American. 1954–

With a limited number of books behind her, Cisneros is nonetheless in the forefront—if not already sitting first chair—of contemporary Hispanic-American fiction writers. The roundly applauded collection of sketches comprising *The House on Mango Street* exemplifies her technique and abilities. The pieces that make up the book are brief, some only four paragraphs in length, none over five pages; there are forty-four in total. These vignettes are minimal, conversational, and anecdotal, told in the first person by Esperanza, a school girl who lives in a Hispanic neighborhood in Chicago. She relates her experiences with and reactions to family, friends, school, and boys; her voice is amusing and poignant, conveying an intuitive and precocious wisdom about life's duplicities and ironies—and occasional rewards. The collection is best read straight through, starting with the first piece—the title of which is the title of the book itself.

Cisneros, Sandra. *The House on Mango Street.* 128p. Random/ Vintage, paper (0-679-73477-5).

CONTEMPORARY MASTERS

Evan Connell
American. 1924–

For many years, Connell was thought of as a "writer's writer"—one whose virtues are appreciated by only a select group of refined readers, most of whom are writers themselves. But he drew wider public notice with the appearance of the 1990 Merchant-Ivory movie *Mr. and Mrs. Bridge,* based on his twin novels *Mrs. Bridge* (1958) and *Mr. Bridge* (1963), which were about an affluent couple in the country-club set of Kansas City. Both novels were rendered in a nontraditional structure: a series of short vignettes. Connell has been an avid writer of short stories throughout his long career, and his mastery of the form was universally recognized upon the 1995 publication of his *Collected Stories.* Connell knows how to tap into typical American characters; he is an extremely insightful observer of human nature, a trait all too obvious in his stories. He is not one to have extended any of the form's frontiers; he certainly exercised it to its finest muscle, though, within its traditional boundaries. He demonstrates a resonant familiarity with history and with foreign places, an accurate ear for dialogue, and a superior aptitude for the use of interior monologue. His prose style is to be admired and studied for its economy, precision, and "just rightness." "Saint Augustine's Pigeon" is definitely his most famous story. Set in New York City, it is about a widower insurance executive's decision to end his celibacy and take a mistress: his descent into hell.

Connell, Evan. *The Collected Stories of Evan S. Connell.* 688p. Counterpoint (1-887178-06-5).

John Cranna
New Zealander. 1954–

Cranna is without extensive publication credits to his name, but his stories have garnered several well-deserved prizes. A surer voice would be difficult to find in a much older writer. His stories are at once lovely and disturbing, with madness—mental imbalance to the point of schizophrenia—being a common theme. His other favorite theme is the wrinkles that spontaneously and unavoidably occur in the fabric of a love/sexual relationship, prohibiting perfect smoothness in the way men and women interact. While often laced with sardonic humor, Cranna's stories consistently show an achingly beautiful empathy with fragile characters. Predictably, he sets his pieces primarily in his South Pacific segment of the world. The title story of the collection *Visitors* serves to introduce the reader not only to this world but also to the author's genius.

Cranna, John. *Visitors*. 133p. Heinemann, paper (0-7900-0050-4).

Deborah Eisenberg
American. 1945–

Enough of Eisenberg's stories have been published in the *New Yorker* to qualify her for the label of a *New Yorker* writer. Her stories have all the urbanity—the tone of sophistication which they are not simply wrapped in but imbued with—that readers expect in a writer often appearing in the hallowed pages of that magazine. Do not assume, however, that she is all verbal dexterity and smug wit; for although many of her stories are set in New York, many are not (some are set even in foreign countries); and they breath with real life, not illusions of life as led on the Upper East Side. All her stories are long; carefully written, they speak of time and consideration in their writing and revision. And this is what Eisenberg is so good at: writing long stories, developing her themes and situations to the fullest, but at the same time writing concisely and sure-handedly, sharply focused on her objective. Never does a story of hers flag or, worse, have the feel of a condensed novel or the outline for a novel that she might have been too lazy to pursue—a sensation readers often get from longer-than-average stories. She writes of contemporary life and its issues, particularly in the arena of love and romantic relationships; she enjoys watching her characters benefit from epiphanous moments, when, usually faced with a crisis, they learn about themselves, especially themselves in some relationship or other. "Transactions in a Foreign Currency" is an exemplary Eisenberg story. A woman, a New Yorker, joins her on-again, off-again lover in Montreal, and although not gaining a firmer grasp on her relationship with the man, ironically she comes away with an unexpected familiarity with a city about which she had no prior knowledge.

Eisenberg, Deborah. *The Stories (So Far) of Deborah Eisenberg.* 419p. Farrar Straus/Noonday, paper (0-374-52492-0).

Mavis Gallant
Canadian. 1922–

Gallant is Montreal-born but of English Protestant heritage. She moved to Europe in the early 1950s, settling in the 1960s in Paris, a place about which she writes authoritatively and atmospherically. She has lived by her writing—the vast majority of her stories finding publication in the *New Yorker*—and the time she has allowed herself to attend to her writing, to say nothing of the impressive talent upon which her efforts rest, has gained her recognition as one of the premier writers of short stories in the world today, only a notch lower than her much-celebrated countrywoman, Alice Munro. Rich language is Gallant's forte, which she displays in long descriptive passages; nothing in terms of either plot or characterization is cut to the bone in a Gallant story. She relishes vivid detail in her presentations of place and human nature. Her stories are psychological portraits, primarily of isolated individuals feeling alien to their surroundings or victimized by it or by other people. She is best at analyzing inner conflicts and their ramifications on behavior. Her sense of structure is impeccable; there is great narrative drive in her stories, in which she presents complete worlds, not simply glimpses. Too, she has a good understanding of the unique experiences of children and young adults. The introductory sentence of the compelling story "The Remission" reveals not only its premise but also Gallant's rich and certainly not overdone style. "When it became clear that Alec Webb was far more ill than anyone had cared to tell him, he tore up his English life and came down to die on the Riviera."

Gallant, Mavis. *The Collected Stories of Mavis Gallant.* 887p. Random (0 679 44886 1).

Gabriel García Márquez
Colombian. 1928–

Short stories are not of incidental status in the oeuvre of this winner of the 1982 Nobel Prize for Literature. He is certainly one of the foremost Latin American fiction writers, one of the foremost proponents of that not uncommon feature in Latin American literature: magic realism, a wondrous mixture of realism and truth-stretching, with humor the glue that holds the two together. Often set in the fictitious Colombian town of Macondo, his stories deal with plain village folk, their goals and frustrations, laced with a handful of fantasy that takes the form of a physically impossible event. For instance, the ironic story, "The Handsomest Drowned Man in the World," concerns a dead man, a total stranger, who washes up onto the beach one day. Villagers find him and are awestruck. How's this for hyperbole? "When they laid him on the floor they said he'd been taller than all other men because there was barely enough room for him in the house, but they thought that maybe the ability to keep on growing after death was part of the nature of certain drowned men." Or this: "They thought that if that magnificent man had lived in the village, his house would have had the widest doors, the highest ceiling, and the strongest floor, his bedstead would have been made from a mid-ship frame held together by iron bolts, and his wife would have been the happiest woman." García Márquez's style is both broad-shouldered and lovely, an irresistible combination.

García Márquez, Gabriel. *Collected Stories.* 320p. HarperPerennial, paper (0-06-091306-1).

Ellen Gilchrist
American. 1935–

Gilchrist is much loved, and understandably so. She is one of the country's best short-story writers, her wonderful yarn-spinning voice having garnered her widespread public appeal. Broadcasting loud and clear is an amiableness, a neighborliness, in her storytelling; the reader gets a sense from a Gilchrist story that she's sitting in a back yard in her native Mississippi and narrating an episode involving some people she knows to a group of avid listeners. Her second collection, *Victory over Japan*, won the 1984 National Book Award and put her on the American short-story map. Her stories, most often set in the South, particularly New Orleans, are satirical, sharp-eyed dramas reflecting contemporary southern culture rather than traditional Old South attitudes and behaviors. As good as she is in scene setting, which she accomplishes swiftly and with minimal but certainly effective detail, it is her characters that glow and sing off the page, especially her female ones. These are forceful characters: indomitable personalities, willful and outspoken in their actions rather than reactions to the world. Her characters operate within a variety of themes and situations; but, regardless, all her stories are tight, intense dramas, each one demonstrating Gilchrist's remarkable ability in the short-fiction form. She is a specialist in compelling, character-revealing dialogue; her insight into how people reveal themselves by what they say is uncanny. She writes in a supple style, clean and lean. Her stories are often laced with violence, and it is shocking when it happens. A case in point is the story "The Gauzy Edge of Paradise." The narrator, Diane, and her friend Lanier, both secretaries to Mississippi state legislators in Jackson, go off to the Gulf coast for time away to practice a diet regimen. They and Diane's male cousin who joins them end up at the mercy of a gun-toting robber who would "just as soon shoot all three of [them] in the face as look at [them]." You laugh and cry at a Gilchrist story.

Gilchrist, Ellen. *Victory over Japan*. 277p. Little, Brown/Back Bay, paper (0-316-31307-6).

Nadine Gordimer
South African. 1923–

The 1991 Nobel Prize winner writes of ordinary themes: love, family, the need for security. But Africa, Africa, *Africa* imbues her writing totally: its vast beauty, its difficult white-black heritage. Gordimer is equally at home creating female and male characters who represent all types found in South African society: from whites in urban centers sensitive to the irony of being a ruling minority, to blacks in townships, to residents of Indian heritage. She practices poised diction, but underneath is a searing commitment to humanity. Her sentences are surface-placid but nonetheless bespeak the racial trouble in her homeland and her passionate intention to see a resolution to the conflict. But Gordimer's stories are not didactic; she does not preach politics. Instead, she hears hearts breaking when skulls are cracked by oppression. "The Chip of Glass Ruby" is a fine example of her social realism, intelligently and straightforwardly rendered.

Gordimer, Nadine. *Selected Stories.* 448p. Penguin, paper (0-14-006737-X).

Allan Gurganus
American. 1947–

North Carolina native Gurganus made a huge splash—striking both the critical and popular imaginations—with the 1988 publication of his first novel, *Oldest Living Confederate Widow Tells All,* which won the Sue Kaufman Prize for First Fiction. And with the publication of his first collection of short stories, *White People,* he proved his mastery over the short form as well. (*White People* won the 1991 *Los Angeles Times* Book Prize for fiction.) Born into the New South though he was, Gurganus, in theme, style, and sensibilities, is still very much rooted in the Old South, very much a child of Eudora Welty, Flannery O'Connor, and William Faulkner. He's got a big, old-fashioned, luxurious style as rich as pecan pie; and what finesse he demonstrates in building beautiful, poetic sentences! He writes about the myths and manners of southern living, all in a clear, gentle, satiric voice that strips back the defensive layers of social convention; but at the same time he is empathetic to human frailties and sympathetic to inadvertent posturing. His stories are at once funny and heartbreaking. Like fellow southern writers, Gurganus chuckles at human nature but fundamentally respects it, too; what is admirable about his stories, also, is his ability to assume a wide variety of points of view. Two of his most embracing stories are "Adult Art" and "Nativity, Caucasian." In the first story, the local superintendent of schools, a married man with children, nonetheless has an "added tenderness": a feeling he gets "from a certain kind of other man." And in this story, we witness his seduction of one of those men. In the second story, the narrator hilariously relates the details of his own birth, which happened all too unexpectedly while his mother attended a bridge party.

Gurganus, Allan. *White People*. 252p. Fawcett Columbine/Ballantine, paper (0-449-91187-X).

Barry Hannah
American. 1942–

As marvelous as Hannah's novels are, in the long term his reputation will probably be defined more by his short stories, a form to which he continues robustly to contribute. His reputation as a master was established with the 1978 publication of the collection *Airships*. He is a writer as closely associated with his native Mississippi as William Faulkner and Eudora Welty. He is certainly one of the most individual voices in contemporary American fiction. In incredibly vivid language, at once rock tough and lovely, Hannah creates a gamut of peculiar characters, but all of them seem to the reader, on second thought, to be no more peculiar than many other representatives of humanity. He peers beneath the surface of social order to find the menace and even violence always threatening to break the surface. His stories are outlandish, violent, hilarious, poignant, and strange to the point of surreal, populated by misfits and damaged souls. His characters deal with, and in some instances revel in, love and desire, craziness and cruelty. Some of his stories are set during the Civil War. Two stories in particular promise to captivate. "Snerd and Niggero" is the tale of an affair in which the woman dies, leaving her lover and husband to become fast friends. In "A Creature in the Bay of Saint Louis," a man remembers his boyhood struggle with the spectacular one that got away.

Hannah, Barry. *High Lonesome*. 240p. Grove/Atlantic, paper (0-8021-3532-3).

Aidan Higgins
Irish. 1927–

A Higgins story wears metaphors stacked up one right after the other, sentence after sentence, without a lot of breathing space in between for the reader to catch up. Each Higgins story shows unusual but vivid word choice: big, strong, unpredictable words that cause the reader to travel slowly down the line of a sentence. Devoid of strong narrative structure, his stories are pieces of character sketch interspersed with moments of rumination on the underside of life. His settings range from Ireland to England to Germany to South Africa; he uses his pen to shine a steady beam of illumination on the dreariness of minds darkened by loneliness or bent on unfortunate choices in life and love. "Killachter Meadow" concerns the old Anglo-Irish aristocracy that used to run Ireland, and the barren lives of four sisters in the last generation of one of those families. Dreary, yes—but arresting, too. The character analysis and verbal dexterity are amazing.

Higgins, Aidan. *Asylum and Other Stories.* 191p. Riverrun Press, paper (0-7145-0230-8).

Francisco Hinojosa

Mexican. 1954–

In Hinojosa's first story collection to be translated into English, he broadcasts his talents to readers north of the Rio Grande, and how appreciative they will be. Every story is a tour de force. Hinojosa tailors each story's structure to suit its particular narrative needs. The short story thrives because of its flexibility, because of the elasticity of its definition; and this creative author manipulates the form with the ease of a master far beyond his years and experience. He sees life as a cycle of ups and downs: mostly downward spirals. His prose style is spare as he strips plots and characterizations to bare bones; but certainly his writing is not bland, for at the same time he luxuriates in rich language. Dark, sarcastic humor simply rises like vapor from his writing. It is difficult to choose favorites from among the major stories in the collection; they are all so splendid. But an example of what Hinojosa can accomplish with knockout results is "An Example of Beauty," a structurally amazing piece. He satirizes the career climb of an artist who wants to create something beautiful and finds fame as a consequence. In the hands of a less able writer, this story would have had the sense of a condensed novel: too much happening over too long a time period in too few pages. But Hinojosa tracks one unifying theme, selecting only the most significant details to develop it, and the results are amusingly satisfying. Other stories to particularly enjoy are "This Time, the War Was Getting Serious" and "Damn Kids."

Hinojosa, Francisco. *Hectic Ethics*. 105p. City Lights, paper (0-87286-347-6).

Thom Jones
American. 1945–

Through three collections of short stories, Jones has both established a reputation as a definite master of the genre and gained increasing popular appeal. This National Book Award finalist and O. Henry Award winner could not be less concerned about writing quiet little domestic dramas in which your peaceful, law-abiding—boring, in other words—neighbors figure. No, he likes loud, nervous characters surviving against the tricky currents of personal affliction (mental or physical) and social trauma. His funny, busy, compelling stories record a great originality and range in the kinds of characters he features and the sorts of situations from which they must extract themselves. He writes a lot about the world of the boxing gym. His characters are working class, the underdog in society's eyes; they're tough guys, often at the mercy of disease and marital distress. Jones is realistic about their gritty lives, writing in an appropriate style: open, aggressive, staccato—but sheer in its ability to conjure the edginess of these guys' lives. "Sonny Liston Was a Friend of Mine" is one of Jones's best stories—and isn't the title terrific, too? Who can resist reading a story so beguilingly titled? Anyway, it's about a young boxer, Kid Dynamite, whose pummeling in the ring serves to keep the real world at bay. Another outstanding story, which shows Jones's range in voices, is "Daddy's Girl," which tells a ninety-two-year-old woman's tale about her sister and their relationship to their abusive, alcoholic father.

Jones, Thom. *Sonny Liston Was a Friend of Mine*. 320p. Little, Brown (0316-47223-9).

Nicholas Jose
Australian. 1952–

Few writers can get as much said, and said as effectively, in such a short space as this Australian. His style is spare, highly burnished. His keen sense of how to mesh what is stated with what is implied allows him to utilize the short story to its most provocative perfection: distilling the crystalline universality of moments in ordinary lives. The story "The Framer" is both the best in this collection and typical of them all. In the short space of eight pages, the rise and fall of a love affair are charted; the essence of the feelings involved is rendered with remarkable resonance. The reader leaves this stunning piece with no doubts as to what the experience was like for the man and woman involved.

Jose, Nicholas. *Feathers or Lead.* 176p. Penguin, paper
(0-14-008851-2).

David Leavitt
American. 1961–

Critics and readers alike look upon Leavitt as one of the premier gay writers working today, while the actual truth about him is simpler and less specific than that: he is an excellent writer, period—gay or otherwise. His first short-story collection, *Family Dancing,* was a finalist for both the National Book Critics Circle Award and the PEN/ Faulkner Award. Various permutations of love and sexual attraction are major themes of his; the aspect of sex and attraction that can be separated out and defined as love, and the part of love that is really sexual attraction, are the areas of personal relationships he is most intrigued with exploring. Dialogue in a Leavitt story is as natural as speech is natural to human beings in the first place. He writes of gay love in the AIDS era, but not despairingly; his voice, at once amusing and serious, implies authority over his subject matter and suggests great empathy for his characters, whether diseased or simply down at heart. All this is delivered in a lyrical, even elegant, style that does nothing but facilitate the reader's enjoyment of his stories. The story "Gravity" has in spades all the properties a very short story must have to succeed in packing a wallop that resonates far beyond the reading of its few pages. Theo is dying of AIDS and has moved back home with his mother, who is consummately supportive and protective. One day they go "shopping for revenge": to get a certain person a better gift than that person had given. For one brief moment during the outing, though, a chink appears in the mother's armor, a crack in her facade of cheerful "bucking up."

Leavitt, David. *A Place I've Never Been.* 194p. Penguin, paper (0-14-010959-5).

Doris Lessing
Rhodesian. 1919–

In Lessing's "The Day Stalin Died," a Communist writer finds herself distracted on the day the Soviet leader passes away by family interruptions and her self-doubt about her true affiliation to the Party. This story offers a good example of the intense social and political consciousness Lessing, briefly a member of the Communist Party herself, brings to her stories. Her socialist leanings show through, as do her concerns for racial and feminist struggles. Settings are Africa and Britain, two familiar personal environments. Characters are mixed—all sorts of people. Lessing is unjubilant in her acute dissections of psychology; she's cerebral, a cool analyzer of the more depressing attitudes found in the heart and mind. Lessing's stories challenge her readers to become more alert to the political ways of people.

Lessing, Doris. *Stories.* 625p. Random, paper (0-394-74249-4).

Bobbie Ann Mason
American. 1940–

Mason established herself very early in her writing career, winning the Ernest Hemingway Foundation Award for first fiction in 1983 for her first short-story collection, *Shiloh and Other Stories.* She represents the writers of the "New South," those who explore contemporary southern life, a life no longer grounded in the Old South customs and issues of William Faulkner and Flannery O'Connor, but one that straddles tradition and modernity. Her characters must cope with both the changes today brings and the traditional constraints and securities of yesterday. Her stories are set mostly in small towns in her native Kentucky and are populated by lower-middle-class people who often lead lives of frustration and confusion but usually see some light, however faint, at the end of the tunnel. She is interested in the tension between rural and urban life as well as between Old South and New. A Mason story scrutinizes contemporary lives of very ordinary people who inhabit a world of shopping malls and interstate highways; her narratives are brimming with brand names and titles of television shows, anchoring themselves very much in today's society. Her characters face unemployment, poverty, awkwardness in attempting any sort of introspection, and family conflicts, including custody of children. Her prose is precisely detailed, and she demonstrates continued ability to handle realistic dialogue. Her voice, it must be said, is relatively flat, but actually it correlates well with the milieu about which she writes. "Shiloh" is her most famous story. A couple's visit to the Shiloh Civil War battlefield symbolizes the opposition that jeopardizes their already strained marriage.

Mason, Bobbie Ann. *Midnight Magic: Selected Stories of Bobbie Ann Mason.* 301p. Ecco (0-88001595-0).

William Maxwell
American. 1908–

Maxwell, a former fiction editor at the *New Yorker,* was born in Lincoln, Illinois. He has written brilliant novels and short stories set in the Midwest in the early twentieth century; this is his best work. Other of his fiction concerns life in New York City and American travelers in Europe seeking to absorb the meaning of what they observe. The reader may initially perceive Maxwell's immaculately styled stories set in the fictional Illinois town of Draperville (read "Lincoln") as indictments of the pettiness of small-town midwestern life; but long before the story is finished, Maxwell's compassion and his detachment in terms of passing judgment are readily apparent. By story's end, the reader sees that Maxwell's midwestern stories are essentially tender expressions of the tenor of life there. Unlike Sherwood Anderson, who viewed the Midwest as a unique place of enforced conformity, Maxwell seeks to extend midwestern experiences into the realm of universal human experiences—to insist that relationships between family and friends (his usual subject matter) bear certain identifiable traits the world over, whether the individuals live in a small or large community. "The Trojan Women" is an illustrative story: a delicate exploration of a small-town marriage gone sour and the wife's paranoia that everyone in town is against her.

Maxwell, William. *All the Days and Nights: The Collected Stories.* 415p. Random/Vintage, paper (0-679-76102-0).

John McGahern
Irish. 1934–

McGahern's stories show his keen sensitivity to the abrupt differences between Ireland's recent past and its present: the difficult transition from rural to industrial society. His stories are built on those particular sociocultural foundations of the past—English domination and the country-versus-city conflict—that bear most heavily on Ireland's present and future. McGahern deals with the kind of people one encounters every day—outwardly ordinary men and women who possess subtleties that, below the surface, mark them as unique in their own way. The exteriors of these stories are quiet and low-key, but their psychological fathomings reach deep waters. Dialogue in most cases carries the plot; people reveal themselves through what they say. McGahern's lyricism is limpid; while he respects economy, he doesn't make the reader trip over brittle brevity.

McGahern, John. *The Collected Stories.* 408p. Random/Vintage, paper (0-679-74401-0).

Michael McLaverty
Irish. 1907–

McLaverty sets his extremely fine stories in Northern Ireland, among rural folk and city people. Their lives are hard, and he renders them realistically: their struggles with emotions toward others, their struggles with the inexorable alterations and adjustments that the passage of time brings. Nevertheless, a gentle tone pervades all his writing.

McLaverty is a precise stylist, always stating his words with economy. He allows one carefully composed sentence to evoke a whole string of significances in both action and emotion. His stories are open-ended, featuring a beguilingly demure reluctance to draw the final conclusion—as if he were saying to the reader, "You do it, because I've already shown you what it will be." "The Schooner" is a poignant story about a young boy's attachment to a model schooner while he's on summer vacation.

McLaverty, Michael. *Collected Stories.* 278p. Dufour Editions, paper (0-905169-14-X).

James Alan McPherson
American. 1943–

McPherson's output is not vast. But he is a fully mature, stunning writer. His stories deal with contemporary black life in the United States, on all socioeconomic levels: blacks alienated from whites as they encounter each other in the workplace or even in bed, blacks alienated from each other because their racial expressions take different tacks. A case in point is the story "The Faithful." John Butler, barber and preacher, is failing at both, unable to get with the times and give people what they want in haircuts or in sermons. McPherson's scrutiny of black lives is stringently realistic but warmed by humor and compassion. He writes in a style of elegant rawness, of precise spontaneity.

McPherson, James Alan. *Elbow Room.* 286p. Ballantine/Fawcett, paper (0-449-21357-9).

Lorrie Moore
American. 1957–

Moore will make you laugh out loud. But she can also be so poignant that she'll bring a tear to your eye. She is certainly one of the strongest voices in the American short story today, and she's a relatively "new" voice, too; in other words, she is tops among those short-story writers who have "come of age" in recent years. In Moore's case, however, she pretty much arrived on the scene fully fledged. Her stories are at once sad and funny, at the same time touching and devastatingly wicked. The reader marvels at her intelligent observations of social predicaments and personality traits. She is exceptional at isolating vitally significant details, which, like little explosions of meaning, go a long way in explaining the nature of a personality or a particular situation. Her stories often explore the terrain of modern relationships; she focuses on lives with bruises, contusions, and even fractures as people stretch to connect with one another, stretch for an understanding of themselves and their relations with others. In addition to her obvious intelligence and her sly, sardonic sense of humor, her prose style is astonishingly original in metaphor and simile. Her characters are easy to identify with; she certainly has her thumb on the pulse of contemporary life, which explains her popularity. Be sure to read "Community Life," one of the best stories to have been written by anyone in recent years. It's about a woman librarian, transplanted from Vermont to the Midwest, and her pain in coming out of herself to give to both her community and a new relationship.

Moore, Lorrie. *Birds of America.* 345p. Knopf (0-679-44597-8).

Bharati Mukherjee
Indian, American resident. 1940–

That Mukherjee could rightfully claim mastery of the short-story form got its public proclamation by her first collection, *The Middleman and Other Stories,* winning the 1988 National Book Critics Circle Award for Fiction. She writes about immigrants to the United States and Canada, based on her own experience; but she focuses on a wide variety of immigrant groups who contribute to the American cultural richness and the diverse fabric of our society. Her characters come from such places as Iraq, the Philippines, and Trinidad; they come to New York, Detroit, and other places. But from wherever they come, wherever they settle, they are determined to be a part of the American experience. The clash of cultures—East and West, Third World and First—is the material from which she spins her very original stories. Mukherjee writes in a deliciously clear prose at once colloquial in its realism and poetic in its concise expressiveness. She is perfectly capable of handling a wide divergence of voices and perspectives, whether male or female. Her stories brim with violence, passion, and wit; ultimately, they are wise, empathetic, and very moving. "The Middleman" is a magnificently complex story about an Iraqi Jew, an immigrant to Queens, New York, who is now, because of shady dealings, living in exile in the Central American jungle; he has inadvertently, because of his penchant for beautiful women, gotten involved in the local revolution. In "Jasmine," the title character journeys from Trinidad to Detroit, leaving her homeland because "Trinidad was an island stuck in the middle of nowhere. What kind of place was that for a girl with ambition?" Her exploitation by employers she interprets as freedom and "getting ahead."

Mukherjee, Bharati. *The Middleman and Other Stories.* 194p.
   Fawcett Crest/Ballantine, paper (0-449-21718-3).

Alice Munro
Canadian. 1931–

The great American writer Robert Penn Warren wrote, in connection with the sterling qualities of the short fiction of his fellow southerner, Katherine Anne Porter, "A story must test its thematic line at every point against its total circumstantiality; the thematic consideration must, as it were, be validated in terms of circumstance and experience." Warren would probably ticket Munro for violating this cardinal rule. In fact, he might have dubbed her "Ramblin' Alice." For instance, "The Royal Beatings," the first story in the cycle of interrelated stories following several decades in the lives of Rose and her stepmother, Flo, serves to introduce the reader to the two women's up-and-down, uneasy relationship to Munro's trademark indirectness of storytelling. She draws in characters and incidents from many points in their relationship, past, present, and future—rather than focusing on one or two incidents to impart the nature of their feelings for each other. Nonetheless, there is in this tendency to digress a naturalness of voice that gives her stories a feel of listening to someone sitting next to you on the bus telling a favorite anecdote. Don't we often ramble, get sidetracked, in trying to "make a long story short?" Munro's style is perfectly plain—perfectly suited to her unaffected storytelling voice—and she has a propensity for dealing with ordinary peoples' inability to communicate effectively, a condition easy for readers to identify with.

Munro, Alice. *Selected Stories*. 545p. Knopf (0-679-44627-3); Random/Vintage, paper (0-679-76674-X).

R. K. Narayan
Indian. 1906–

Narayan's stories are microcosms of village life in contemporary India; within both broad social contexts (the rigidity of class lines, the consummate interest village people have in each other's business) and on strictly personal levels (individuals' confrontations with the raw deals life hands them and how they cope). Narayan's stories are populated with a range of characters, from holy men to astrologers to children. He relies heavily on plot, but his plots are compressed to a few pages—so that the very process of the story's compactness sends off sparks of pungency. Narayan's humorous stories are written in a simple, naive tone—fablelike, as if at the end a moral will be pointed out. "A Horse and Two Goats" memorably details a funny encounter between a goatherd and an American tourist.

Narayan, R. K. *The Grandmother's Tale and Other Stories*. 312p. Ecco, paper (0-88001-624-8).

Joyce Carol Oates
American. 1938–

Admirably or maddeningly prolific—depending on one's point of view—Oates is undeniably not a consistent writer. In her short stories, especially, she can write a dead sentence and create a tired plot; or she can write a lyrical sentence and create a buoyant plot. She can string a story out to flabbiness or make it perfectly taut. As is the case with several fiction writers past and present, Oates gives her sensibility sharper expression in the short-story form than in her novels. Violence and sexual tension are typical Oates themes; people frustrated by the latter, leading to the former; people alienated from their environment. Her stories are set anywhere—urban, suburban, rural—and she is a master of dialogue. "Where Are You Going, Where Have You Been?" presents the essence of Oates the story writer. Connie is an ordinary, dreamy teenage girl. To her door one day comes Arnold, hardly the knight-in-shining armor she'd been expecting. (Her novel *them* won the 1970 National Book Award.)

Oates, Joyce Carol. *Where Are You Going, Where Have You Been?: Selected Early Stories.* 522p. Ontario Review, paper (0-865-38078-3).

Edna O'Brien
Irish. 1930–

O'Brien writes about her native land and London (her residence for several years) and primarily about love, sex, and women: their romantic needs, their sexual natures, their conflicts with men. Also, in many instances, she writes of childhood in Ireland viewed through the distancing lens of adult relocation to another land. Regardless of theme or subject matter, O'Brien always displays an open, honest heart, leaving the reader to almost wince at her candor. But there is nothing sentimental or cloying in her work. Her style is lush yet exacting, full of kinetic energy, her stories consistently gritty, both emotionally and sensually. A lot of pain and hurt is involved in an O'Brien story. "The Creature" concerns an unfortunate woman in a town in the west of Ireland whom everyone refers to as "The Creature."

O'Brien, Edna. *A Fanatic Heart: Selected Stories of Edna O'Brien.* 480p. NAL/Dutton, paper (0-452-26116-3).

Juan Carlos Onetti
Uruguayan. 1909–

In the novel and short-story forms, Uruguay has made significant contributions to twentieth-century literature; and one of the most important Uruguayan short-story writers of this century is Juan Carlos Onetti. Onetti spent the first twenty years of his life in his native Uruguay, followed by a residency in Argentina, and then, for political reasons, exile in Spain. He won the 1962 Uruguayan National Prize for Literature. In his stories he explores the urban environment, focusing on the paradox of the solitary soul living in towns and cities. Often his stories are set in the fictional town of Santa Maria, mean home to sordid existences and failed prospects—a microcosm for his analysis of the burst-dream syndrome that has marked Latin American history. Onetti's acknowledged master is William Faulkner, after whom he patterned his somewhat elaborate style (although Onetti's writing is, actually, much more fluid than his Mississippi hero's notoriously difficult prose) and his creation of a complete, imaginary world in the town of Santa Maria (à la Yoknapatawpha County). His stories exist in a sphere where fantasy, absurdity, and realism mutually dwell; what his characters are up to, and the plights they appear to be involved in, are always ambiguously presented. A case in point is the story "The House on the Sand," wherein a recurrent Onetti character, Dr. Diaz Grey, relates a strange beachside incident with a seductive woman and a man reminiscent of Lennie from Steinbeck's *Of Mice and Men*—all of which is refracted through the distorting lens of memory.

Onetti, Juan Carlos. *Goodbyes and Stories*. 174p. University of Texas, paper (0-292-72746-1).

Cynthia Ozick
American. 1928–

Ozick claims the essay as her favorite literary form, and, indeed, she is one of the premier contemporary American essayists. But her short stories earn her great respect from critics as well as from the reading public. Her short stories are grounded in Yiddish folklore; they arise from Jewish religious and cultural traditions and explore, either literally or figuratively, various elements of Jewish law and history. Her extreme intelligence is obvious in her wordplay and in the philosophic, psychological, and religious ideas she investigates in the course of her storytelling. Thematically, Ozick is often concerned with the clash of cultures between Jews and Christians. Her characters are often beset by misunderstanding, loneliness, or distractedness. Many of her short stories are comic satires and often lampoon the Jewish literary culture in the United States. Her prose is highly stylized, and with her stories' rhetorical and structural diversity, readers will not find them straightforward in development. But they will find Ozick's wittiness perfectly charming, which gives her stories appeal to the heart as well as the intellect. "The Pagan Rabbi" draws together Ozick's major thematic concerns and showcases her particular stylistic and development peculiarities. A rabbi friend of the narrator hangs himself from a tree in a public park. The widow attempts to convince the narrator that her late husband was not a scholar or a remarkable Jew but a pagan. Complicated, challenging, but truly captivating.

Ozick, Cynthia. *The Pagan Rabbi and Other Stories.* 270p. Syracuse University, paper (0-8156-0351-7).

Grace Paley
American. 1922–

Paley has written very little, but her critical reputation is high. She is a lean writer, avidly avoiding excessive description. She writes little sarcastic social comedy-dramas set in New York, mostly about vulnerable women—divorced or separated, yet still needing and depending on men. Dialogue, without quotation marks, carries the plot, and very little happens outside of what people say to each other. Paley's ability to reproduce vocal inflections on the printed page is uncanny. "Wants" is a good story to begin with: four pages, a first-person narrator. A woman encounters her ex-husband one day. Then she ponders the passage of time. Despite its brevity, a thought-provoking piece.

Paley, Grace. *The Collected Stories.* 386p. Farrar (0-374-12636-4); Farrar/Noonday, paper (0-374-52431-9).

Jayne Anne Phillips
American. 1952–

Phillips hasn't written short stories in quite some time, but despite that, and regardless of how well her novels written in the meantime have been received, she will always remain primarily a short-story writer in the minds of the reading public. Her National Book Critics Circle Award-winning collection *Black Tickets* put her on the literary map; it is the book most people associate with her and react to most strongly. She writes about love, sexuality, alienation, family dysfunction, street life, and middle-class values. Her specialty in *Black Tickets* is short monologues, which average two or three pages in length. A good example is "Blond Girls," in which a party of girls, in a shack "down the hill," get drunk on wine and tell each other scary stories, and are watched by a group of local boys. This brief story, and others such as "Mammasita," in which a colorful character goes out every night to chase drunks into the Social Care Center, may initially strike readers as sketches too brief to truly engage their attention; they may seem little more than self-conscious exercises of "poetic" language for its own sake. But don't dismiss Phillips's short pieces so easily. The vital truths they tell about life will resonate in the reader's mind far, far longer than the few minutes it took to read the short number of pages they fill. And in her longer stories, such as "Home," she is sublime at psychological realism. This trenchant, moving story concerns a young woman's return to her family home. "I ran out of money and I wasn't in love, so I have come home to my mother," she says; and the story is about the two of them attempting to establish an equilibrium as two adult women living in the same close quarters.

Phillips, Jayne Anne. *Black Tickets.* 265p. Delta/Bantam Doubleday
    Dell, paper (0-385-28088-2).

James Plunkett
Irish. 1920–

"The Half-Crown" is an absolutely endearing story, poignant without being precious. It concerns a young man in Dublin—where Plunkett sets his stories—who is in desperate need of some money to entertain a girl he's sweet on. But when a half-crown comes into his possession illicitly, he has a change of heart on spending it the way he had intended. Like many Irish short-story writers, Plunkett sorts through contemporary life and finds intellectual and experiential narrowness. His stories reflect the economic and social frustration of his native land, as felt by men and women not blessed with birthright or money. There is intelligent sentiment at play in a Plunkett story—

he quietly appreciates the short distance between heart and mind in the cause of motivation.

Plunkett, James. *Collected Short Stories*. 299p. Poolberg Press, Dublin, Ireland, paper (0-905169-10-7).

Reynolds Price
American. 1933–

Short story writer, novelist, playwright, poet, essayist, memoirist— North Carolina's Price is among the best contemporary southern American writers. No, among the best American writers, period. His first novel, *A Long and Happy Life,* was published in 1962 to loud critical applause; and it is this novel and the several astounding ones that followed that are the wellspring of his reputation for brilliance. (His novel *Kate Vaiden* won the 1986 National Book Critics' Circle Award.) Nonetheless, his short stories share with the novels a radiance not to be overlooked. Price's fiction gives the impressions of having been derived from the stories families tell about themselves. Specifically, he writes about people searching for love from parents and from the opposite or the same sex; and reaching for a satisfactory personal identity in their own eyes and in others' eyes. Sadly, some readers don't care for Price. What impedes their enjoyment of him is his elaborate style: too baroque (in their estimation) to read easily. How wrong-headed! Granted, Price is no minimalist; he's the difference between a superhighway and an elegant old elm-lined, brick-paved boulevard. He is a celebrator of the ability of language not only to express but to express breathtakingly; consequently, a joy to savor. A case in point is the story "A Dog's Death." Why is this brief piece so extremely affecting? Because it couches intense but honest emotion in unabashed language.

Price, Reynolds. *The Collected Stories*. 625p. Atheneum (0-689-12147-4); Plume, paper (0-452-27218-1).

James Purdy
American. 1923–

Purdy has been a prolific writer, producing many novels, collections of short stories, poetry, and plays. But he has been to a large extent critically ignored, and popular audiences have never flocked to his work. But his stories, at least, deserve a readership for their sheer effectiveness. Purdy certainly has a dark view of life; to him, life is nothing but tragic. And he expresses his particularly dark view of life in various manifestations of human behavior: the inability of individuals to communicate and connect, people's ineptitude in coping with what they desire from life, suppressed and unexpressed love and sexuality, the self-destructive family, and domestic violence, even perpetuated by children. This last situation is found in his most famous story, "The Color of Darkness." The wife of a young married man ran away years ago, leaving him with a young son; and the man is distressed because he can't remember how his wife looked, particularly the color of her eyes. The connection with her was so brief, and now he is discovering his relationship with his little son emotionless. The way the boy acts out his need for his father's attention makes a strong ending to this story. Another of Purdy's major themes is homoeroticism, which is developed to full bloom in "Lily's Party," in which two men have taken possession of a woman in an isolated cottage and then fall to addressing their own mutual desire. Despite the darkness or even sordidness of Purdy's stories, his style is always "soft": tight, even-flowing sentences, rendered in the way most people actually speak.

Purdy, James. *63: Dream Palace: Selected Stories 1956–1987.* 352p.
    Black Sparrow, paper (0-87685-844-2).

Salman Rushdie
Indian. 1947–

No one would suggest that Rushdie is primarily a short-story writer, but his first and thus far only collection of stories nonetheless put him on the short-story map. Whether Rushdie is safe abroad in the world remains to be seen. Who can be certain someone still is not intent on fulfilling the sentence of death he incurred in the Muslim world by the publication of his explosive 1989 novel, *Satanic Verses?* Rushdie's fans have appreciated his stories upon their initial publication in such magazines as the *New Yorker* and the *Atlantic,* and they now have them brought together within the covers of one book, to be enjoyed in their collective impressiveness. The overarching theme is the clash and cooperation between Eastern and Western cultures. The nine stories are arranged into three groupings, labeled "East," "West," and "East, West." The Eastern ones have a *Thousand and One Nights* flavor to them and are set in Rushdie's native India. The best among this grouping is "Good Advice Is Rarer Than Rubies," about a young woman who goes to the British consulate for a visa so she may live with her husband; her charm defeats the old man she encounters at the door, who wants to supply her with fraudulent papers. Rushdie's Western stories incorporate elements of magic realism and feature European settings. The most compelling is "Christopher Columbus and Queen Isabella of Spain Consummate Their Relationship," giving the affiliation between the encounterer of the New World and the Castilian queen a definite sexual angle. The stories in the "East, West" section bring the two worlds together, and the outstanding one of that beautiful trio is "The Harmony of the Spheres," about a deeply felt but tragically ended friendship between an Englishman and an Indian. Rushdie's brilliant style reinforces his stories' marvelous combination of dignity and poignancy. The entire world is Rushdie's terrain, and his knowledge of it is wide and deep; as his stories so explicity reveal, he is one of the most cosmopolitan writers in the business today.

Rushdie, Salman. *East, West: Stories.* 224p. Pantheon (0-679-43965-X).

J. D. Salinger
American. 1919–

The author of the classic 1951 coming-of-age novel *Catcher in the Rye* is now equally famous for his reclusiveness. Salinger is also a superior short-story writer. Many of his stories feature the Glass family of New York, an Irish-Jewish theatrical family. He often writes about children or adolescents but also about married couples. His characters strike the reader as neurotic, alienated, and lacking in communication skills. But he can write about them with much humor. His well-regarded stories were written decades ago but still seem fresh and creative. "A Perfect Day for Bananafish" is a much-loved as well as representative example; it is part of Salinger's Glass family cycle of stories. It is set in 1948, and the details of that period definitely give it an "old" feeling to contemporary readers; but it remains as engaging piece of work. A young woman is staying at a hotel in Florida. In the story's first part, she's on the phone with her mother, and they have a beautifully authentic dialogue: beautifully authentic in that it accurately reflects the way people actually converse. It becomes apparent that she's come here on a vacation with her mentally unstable husband. In the story's second part, her husband, Seymour Glass, is on the beach talking to a little girl. Again, we are witness to outstandingly authentic dialogue; even the little girl's speech patterns are right on the money in terms of sheer realism. Seymour relates perfectly to the little friend. Is he really mentally disturbed? We hardly believe so now. In part three of the story, though, we must reach that conclusion, for he goes back into their hotel room and shoots himself in the temple. Outstanding in both technique and effect.

Salinger, J. D. *Nine Stories*. 198p. Little, Brown, paper
(0-316-76950-9).

James Salter
American. 1925–

Salter's one and only collection of short stories—thus far, anyway— won the 1992 PEN/Faulkner Award. And it's no wonder. What a stunning collection it is; what a skilled story writer Salter reveals himself to be. But even with his award-winning collection and several novels to his credit, he continues to operate in relative obscurity in the eyes of the general reading public. He's not widely read; his proficiencies are too underrated. That is not as it should be; the truth is, he is a flawless practitioner of compression; that is, the capability of the significant detail to suggest much more than meets the eye, and the ability of simple language to move the reader's emotions neatly and efficiently. He offers the barest outline of context for his stories, only what we need to know about the setting and characters involved; his sense of structure, though, is impeccable. He makes minimal presentation sing with resounding resonance; it's not easy to forget a Salter story. Thematically speaking, his work often springs from the tensions between men and women. Typical Salter style and theme are in full display in the first story in the collection, "Am Strande von Tanger," its beautiful spareness obvious from the opening lines: "Barcelona at dawn. The hotels are dark. All the great avenues are pointing to the sea." The story concerns a young American artist living in that Spanish city. One day he and his girlfriend and her friend go to the beach; in their absence, their caged bird dies, an event not too difficult for them to read as symbolic of the true nature of their own relationship. Another interesting story is "Via Negativa," a revealing story about obscure writers and famous ones.

Salter, James. *Dusk and Other Stories*. 157p. Farrar/North Point, paper (0-86547-389-7).

Alan Sillitoe
English. 1928–

Sillitoe made his name with his first novel, *Saturday Night and Sunday Morning* (1958), but his mark on English literature has been made more permanent by his short stories, which, in their concentrated effect, achieve a lyrical beauty generally missing from his novels. Sillitoe is of a working-class background in Nottingham, and it is this milieu he so successfully explains and even exploits in his fiction. Rendered in his trademark streetwise vernacular, his coarsely realistic stories piquantly evoke the geography of industrial northern England and the psychology found down those mean lanes. Sillitoe writes with an abiding social consciousness: for him, the determining factor in English community life—whether there is to be personal advancement through it or not—is social class; and his characters are usually in revolt against the established political, economic, and social agencies in their lives. His characters tend to defy authority; they assert their individualism. The "outsider" is the person Sillitoe writes about; rebellion, isolation, and alienation are the fields he tills. This is no more apparent than in his classic story "The Loneliness of the Long-Distance Runner," which is widely anthologized. It is the unforgettable tale of a young man in reform school, chosen to compete in a long-distance race, who, even in the face of achieving victory for the first time in his life, is not about to "reform."

Sillitoe, Alan. *Collected Stories*. 585p. HarperCollins (0-06-255570-0).

Lee Smith
American. 1944–

Smith's delectable southern yarniness could not be more hospitable. She writes of people next door, with people-next-door plights—but writes about them empathetically and humorously. Her characters are people trying to maintain their place in life, however modest that place may be; people who keep their dignity in the face of others' wrongheaded perceptions about them; and people trying to smooth out domestic disharmonies. Her stories are most often first-person narratives told by southern women. Smith writes "confessional" stories: her characters are always getting something off their chests. Her stories may strike some readers as too cutesy, too "cornpone." But no one can deny their wit, the well-observed and telling detail with which each is brimming, or the fact that beneath their popular entertainment surfaces lies a perfect structure. "Between the Lines" is a quintessential piece of Smith storytelling. Mrs. Joline B. Newhouse writes a "fortnightly" column for her local newspaper, in which she "look[s] on the bright side of life." In the course of this yarn, she relates recent and past events in her life that bring her to ask the question "Now where will it all end? I ask you. All this pain and loving, mystery and loss." It's a hilarious story.

Smith, Lee. *Cakewalk*. 256p. Ballantine, paper (0-345-41042-4).

Elizabeth Spencer
American. 1921–

Spencer is a southerner, but unlike many of her compatriots, she often sets her fiction in places other than the American South, places she knows just as familiarly as her home turf, though—namely, Italy and Canada. In "The White Azalea" all of Spencer's qualities can be observed. The story is derived from both of Spencer's worlds, her native Mississippi and abroad. Miss Theresa Stubblefield has devoted her life to being the family nurse; it's always been up to her to tend to the sick and the dying and the bereft in the family. Finally, though, she's realized her real ambition—a trip to Europe. But even there her responsibilities catch up to her in the form of two letters from back home filling her in on the latest family tragedy. As Theresa sits on the Spanish Steps in Rome with the letters in hand, she feels the net-work—the net—of family ties attempting to draw her away from her life's adventure back to being the selfless soul that is her role at home. Theresa, though, breaks out of the spider's web by tearing up the letters and burying them in the soil in a potted azalea decorating the Spanish Steps. Spencer is at her best when limning such a char-acter as Miss Theresa Stubblefield: one of apparently delicate sensi-bilities but, when the truth be told, with a willfulness after all. Spencer is un-Faulknerian in her straightforward, clear style and her linear plot exposition; although perhaps not as "literary" as that great southerner, she's a fine yarn spinner.

Spencer, Elizabeth. *The Light in the Piazza and Other Italian Tales.* 342p. University Press of Mississippi (0-87805-836-2); paper (0-87805-837-0).

Wallace Stegner
American. 1909–

A well-honored fiction writer—winner of prizes, fellowships, and critical applause—Stegner is better known for his novels, which include *The Big Rock Candy Mountain* (1943), *The Angle of Repose* (which won the 1972 Pulitzer Prize), and *The Spectator Bird* (1976), than his short stories. But the 1990 retrospective of his short fiction, pulling together thirty-one stories covering his long and distin-guished career, loudly broadcasts his high level of accomplishment in the shorter form. A master of the effortlessly beautiful metaphor, Stegner writes in a lush but never mannered style. His stories are brief yet do not hint of abbreviation or truncation; there is a sense of spa-ciousness and expansiveness in each story's few pages, arising from the author's ability to create with well-chosen phrases quick but com-plete portraits and concise but fully engrossing narratives. Stegner's abiding interest in the American West permeates his work, as does his consciousness of the influence of the past on people's present lives. "The Berry Patch" is quintessential Stegner, presenting a farm couple going berry picking and capturing the subtle but important commu-nication that transpires between them during those few hours.

Stegner, Wallace. *The Collected Stories of Wallace Stegner.* 525p.
   Penguin, paper (0-14-014774-8).

Paul Theroux
American. 1941–

Theroux has lived and traveled all over the world; his travel books
are marvelous, several of them already considered modern classics of
the genre. His cosmopolitanism is also reflected in his short stories,
readers of which will be amazed at the range of locales he employs
as settings—writing about each one with equal truth and authority.
Despite the fame his travel books have garnered, the applause with
which each new novel of his is greeted popularly and critically,
Theroux possesses definite instincts for the special nature of the
short story. In the introduction to his *Collected Stories,* he relates: "In
a novel I try to make each chapter as complete and harmonious as a
story. My travel books are a sequence of traveler's tales." In an elegant
prose style, he writes in his stories about a variety of people, from
colonials to diplomats to academics. He is a special writer in terms
of his ability to conjure the sights, sounds (including an unerring ear
for dialogue), and sensations found in any locale in which he sets a
story. There is always a sensuality in a Theroux story: in richness of
setting, in spoken or even unspoken sexuality between characters.
Most of his plot situations derive from psychological and cultural
predicaments, often alienation and depression. But through his stories runs, too, a strong vein of comedy. An exemplary story is
"Conspirators," which is set in the Malaysian community of Ayer
Hitan. The narrator works for the foreign service of, presumably, the
United States. He is advised by his superiors to interview a certain
Rao, a local rabble rouser, to "see what he was up to" after having
been released from prison, having served a seven-year sentence. The
narrator finds that Rao "had no fire. I had suspected him of keeping
something from me; but he hadn't, he was concealing nothing, he
had been destroyed." In his official report back home, the narrator
"put down the obvious facts and . . . invented a happy man, whom
prison had cured of all passions."

Theroux, Paul. *The Collected Stories.* 660p. Penguin, paper
   (0-14-027494-4).

William Trevor
Irish. 1928–

Trevor has written many novels and, unlike many other short-story writers who have done so, has been very successful at it; he obviously understands the differences between and integrities of each form. He was raised in Ireland, where he earned a degree at prestigious Trinity College in Dublin. Upon his marriage in 1952, he moved to England, where he has lived ever since. He is considered one of the best short-story writers currently writing in the English language. His stories, like his novels, are set in his native Ireland or in England; they are very traditional narratives, with well-marked beginnings and endings and all stops in between. He relishes the significant detail that in accumulation, like brickwork, builds a strong edifice. Trevor is fascinated with eccentricity; he adeptly dissects the psychology of the strange, eccentric character, from diverse social strata, from child to elder, from shopkeeper to landed gentle folk. He writes in a tragicomic vein with no fancy footwork, only honest pursuit of the truth, love and its rewards and pains, and the frustrations in life that people keep hidden. He often writes of loneliness and disappointment, but he is always sympathetic to his characters' plights. He is an absolute master at concisely yet completely evoking characters and atmospheres. His stories are beautifully sculpted. In 1977 Trevor was named an honorary Commander of the British Empire for his service to literature. "Going Home" is vintage Trevor: about a teenage schoolboy and his teacher riding the same train as they go home on break.

Trevor, William. *The Collected Stories.* 1,261p. Penguin, paper (0-14-023245-1).

John Updike
American. 1932–

The landscape of marriage, particularly the fault lines along which stress and, eventually, cracks will occur, is what Updike explores best in his fiction. That he is an even finer story writer than novelist may become, at some point in the future, the standard critical opinion. Updike's propensity to meander and lecture, readily observable in his novels (though stimulating in its own way), is constrained by the space limitations of the short story; consequently, his brilliance as a writer is expressed in its purest form. The true essence of what lies in the hearts of people is in immaculate focus here. His style, too, is at its best in his stories: the careful rhythm of his syntax and his thoughtful choice of high-impact but smoothly flowing images all add up to beautiful sentences. The sequence called *Too Far to Go: The Maples Stories* tracks, unforgettably, the decline of a suburban middle-class marriage.

Updike, John. *Too Far to Go: The Maples Stories.* 256p. Fawcett, paper (0-449-20016-7).

Eudora Welty
American. 1909–

By virtue of her age combined with the highest of critical esteem and widespread fondness among the reading public, Welty, the grande dame of American fiction writers, is frequently proclaimed the best living American short-story writer. The power of her intelligence, partnered with the charm of her idiosyncratic, off-beat, or untrammeled characters, is an unbeatable match. Welty writes of rural and small-town Mississippi, of lower and middle-class whites and of blacks. A Welty sentence is metaphorically profound and syntactically exacting, thus usually requiring a slow pace. Loneliness is one of the pervasive themes found in her stories; others include love and what a sense of community brings to an individual. Her stories are often comedies, often fantasies, often modern retellings or interpretations of classical myths. Her dialogue is rich and unerring in its control of the vernacular. Like two other southern female authors, Flannery O'Connor and Carson McCullers, Welty also writes of grotesques: people on the other side of total social acceptability due to physical, mental, or behavioral detriments. She is, however, able to distil the veracity of her characters' existence more deeply than her fellow writers. "Why I Live at the P.O." is a favorite of many readers. It's a hilarious story about why Sister, the narrator, decided to go live at the post office, where she works, when her sister returns home.

Welty, Eudora. *The Collected Stories of Eudora Welty.* 576p.
Harcourt, paper (0-15-618921-6).

John Edgar Wideman
American. 1941–

The title story of Wideman's short-story collection *Fever* not only
demonstrates the sobering eloquence of his voice in picturing various elements in the constant friction between black and white soci-
eties in America, but also why he's considered an up-and-comer
who's pretty much arrived. The very unusual, very effecting "Fever"
reaches back into the annals of Philadelphia history to a yellow fever
epidemic that hit that city in the last decade of the eighteenth century.
Rather obliquely told in a series of impressions of Philadelphia's
fetidness in the grips of a fatal disease, from the point of view of a
black pastor tending the ill and the dying and the bereft survivors,
the story recreates the bigoted atmosphere surrounding the civic crisis. "We [the black population] were proclaimed carriers of the fever
and treated as pariahs," the pastor says. As richly upholstered in a
poetic, metaphoric style as they are sturdily framed in rock-hard
intelligence, Wideman's painful stories are, like the fiction of the
great James Baldwin, both loud and beautiful.

Wideman, John Edgar. *Fever: Twelve Stories.* 161p. Penguin, paper
(0-14-014347-5).

Tobias Wolff
American. 1945–

Wolff has written in, and excelled at, several forms. His memoir of
Vietnam (where, from 1964 to 1968, he served in the Army Special
Forces), *In Pharaoh's Army,* was a finalist for the National Book
Award. His memoir of childhood, *This Boy's Life,* won the *Los Angeles
Times* Book Award in 1989. And the novella *The Barracks Thief*
received the PEN/Faulkner Award. But as is the case with so many
fiction writers, his talents are more effectively showcased in the short
story. Wolff's direct, plain, but powerfully expressive style radiates
from his stories like white heat. ("Sweet, almost unbreathable smells
rose from the earth," is a beautiful line from the story "Soldier's

Pay.") He writes about a wide variety of character types, about their vulnerabilities and unpredictabilities, about the experience of love and betrayal between family and friends. His characters are real and are involved in real situations, facing dilemmas we can all relate to. These people lead ordinary lives, but what Wolff does, and does so deceptively easily, is to isolate a moment in their ordinariness that makes their lives at once unique and universal. His stories are commanding in their ostensible simplicity, beneath the surface of which lie immaculate truths about the human condition. His stories are easy to read but difficult to forget: not easy to quit thinking about. Spare, clean, clear imagery compels the reader through the narrative. An outstanding story is the aforementioned "Soldier's Pay," set on a military base; Hooper has been demoted once again, from corporal to private first class. His current duty is to drive the guards around to their various stations, and one night one guard goes a little too edgy and, when another guard shoots him dead, a conspiracy of silence must be planned.

Wolff, Tobias. *Back in the World.* 212p. Random/Vintage, paper (0-679-76796-7).

Anthologies

Anthologies of short stories are great resources for gaining acquaintance with a variety of writers, for discovering whose work doesn't particularly move you and whose demands further investigation. The recent anthologies listed here are outstanding, featuring the works of many writers not previously discussed.

The Art of the Tale: An International Anthology of Short Stories,
    1945–1985. Edited by Daniel Halpern. 832p. Penguin, paper
    (0-14-007949-1).

    Halpern, for many years editor of the esteemed literary journal
    Antaeus, has gathered more than eighty examples of stories written since World War II. What makes this anthology so unique is its scope—not only are traditional stories matched with experimental ones, but the geographical range is superb. U.S. and European short-story writers are here, of course, but the Third World is heavily represented as well.

The Best American Short Stories of the Century. Edited by John
    Updike and Katrina Kenison. 800p. Houghton (0-395-84368-5).

    The distinguished Best American Short Story series has been around for nearly a century, and guest editor Updike and series editor Kenison have culled from the pages of the individual volumes, from each year of the series' existence, a magnificent assortment of outstanding short stories. "Best" is, of course, subjective, but there can be no disputing the superiority of what is presented here.

APPENDIX

The Oxford Book of Short Stories. Edited by V. S. Pritchett. Oxford, paper (0-19-282113-X).

The late, great short-story writer Pritchett assembled this indispensible anthology of forty-one short stories written in the English language over the past two hundred years. It is an outstanding sampling of writers everyone should be aware of to be familiar with the short story. Represented are writers from England, Ireland, Scotland, the United States, New Zealand, Australia, Canada, and India.

Author Index

Nationality Index

American
  Abott, Lee, 84
  Adams, Alice, 23
  Anderson, Sherwood, 24
  Baldwin, James, 25
  Bambara, Toni Cade, 26
  Barthelme, Donald, 27
  Bass, Rick, 86
  Beattie, Anne, 87
  Berriault, Gina, 28
  Bierce, Ambrose, 29
  Bowles, Paul, 31
  Boyle, Kay, 32
  Boyle, T. Coraghessan, 88
  Bradbury, Ray, 89
  Brodkey, Harold, 32
  Caldwell, Erskine, 33
  Carver, Raymond, 35
  Cather, Willa, 36
  Chabon, Michael, 89
  Cheever, John, 36
  Chopin, Kate, 37
  Cisneros, Sandra, 90
  Connell, Evan, 91
  Crane, Stephen, 41
  Dubus, Andre, 43
  Eisenberg, Deborah, 92
  Faulkner, William, 43
  Fisher, Dorothy Canfield, 44
  Fisher, Rudolph, 45
  Fitzgerald, F. Scott, 45
  Freeman, Mary E. Wilkins, 46
  Gilchrist, Ellen, 94
  Gordon, Caroline, 47
  Gurganus, Allan, 96
  Hannah, Barry, 97
  Hawthorne, Nathaniel, 48
  Hemingway, Ernest, 48
  Henry, O., 49
  Hughes, Langston, 50

Hurston, Zora Neale, 51
Irving, Washington, 52
Jackson, Shirley, 52
James, Henry, 53
Jewett, Sarah Orne, 54
Jones, Thom, 99
Lardner, Ring, 57
Leavitt, David, 100
London, Jack, 59
Malamud, Bernard, 60
Mason, Bobbie Ann, 101
Maxwell, William, 102
McCullers, Carson, 62
McPherson, James Alan, 104
Moore, Lorrie, 104
Morris, Wright, 65
Oates, Joyce Carol, 107
O'Connor, Flannery, 68
O'Hara, John, 70
Ozick, Cynthia, 109
Paley, Grace, 110
Parker, Dorothy, 70
Phillips, Jayne Anne, 110
Poe, Edgar Allan, 72
Porter, Katherine Anne, 72
Price, Reynolds, 112
Purdy, James, 112
Salinger, J. D., 114
Salter, James, 115
Smith, Lee, 117
Spencer, Elizabeth, 117
Stafford, Jean, 77
Stegner, Wallace, 118
Steinbeck, John, 78
Taylor, Peter, 80
Theroux, Paul, 119
Twain, Mark, 81
Updike, John, 120
Welty, Eudora, 121
Wescott, Glenway, 81

NATIONALITY INDEX

Subject Index

SUBJECT INDEX

SUBJECT INDEX

Brad Hooper is Associate Editor for *Booklist* magazine, ALA's distinguished review journal for public and school libraries. Brad holds a Master of Science in Library Science and served as reference librarian in the History Department of the Cleveland Public Library before coming to *Booklist*. His short stories, essays, and reviews have appeared in a number of national publications.